I can't actually remember the first time I met Marylou Badeaux ... but I also can't actually remember a time that she wasn't around for the "important" events.

Marylou breezed in & out of Paisley Park and on & off the road. It was probably the Purple Rain Tour, because that's where it all started for me!

Having Marylou in the picture was a refreshing change from working with other "label" people; she fit in, she was a part of the team and inner-circle, and she was always welcome by the entire staff, and Prince. Often times when I'd give Prince a message ... "Prince, so-and-so called..." he'd ignore me completely or say "What did they want?" But, when I'd say "Prince, Marylou phoned," he'd say "Can you get her on the phone for me!" Gladly!

Karen Krattinger

General Manager – Paisley Park

Executive Assistant to Prince

1984–1989

Moments
Remembering Prince

By Marylou Badeaux

Foreword by Eric Leeds

Includes exclusive, never-before-published photographs taken inside Paisley Park in the 1980s!

About image quality: Some photographs and images are of inferior quality due to when they were taken, the camera used, or condition of the item. Rather than leaving these out of the book, I felt images of reduced quality were better than having no images of certain historic moments or items.

Cover Design: Marylou Badeaux and Celeste Mookherjee
Cover Artwork: Mal Bray
Artwork based on photograph by Penner (CC BY-SA 3.0) http://flickr.com/photos/penner/2450784866
Editor: Celeste Mookherjee

Quotes from Friends of Prince and Paisley Park

Marylou Badeaux has the word "bad" in her name, meaning she was the baddest Warner Brothers marketing agent on the planet. This memoir has the stories and photos that have never been heard or seen before from the perspective of someone involved around the inner workings of Prince's world. I definitely think he would've enjoyed all of the memories contained within.   — *Dr. Fink*

Book was a great idea. Really captures the fun, warmth, humor we shared "on the inside".   — *Alan Leeds*

What a great book! You have managed to capture Prince and all the escapades perfectly! Of course, I really love the chapter about the floor heaters. I'm laughing as hard now as I was that day!! It was a Prince moment that has become legendary to the "insiders".

— *Billy Sparks*

I can think of no one better to share stories and perspective from the roller coaster ride that was "Prince" than Marylou. I had the pleasure of experiencing both Prince's legacy and Marylou's passion for his art, first hand for the entirety of both of their careers. Marylou not only witnessed the genius at work and play but also crafted marketing strategies for one of the most incredible, successful, and influential careers in music history.

From enigma, to pop Superstar, to movie star... we, as fans, got to see and hear the talent; Marylou made the process seamless in a business where corporate practices rarely match high-level creativity.

From the casual fan of pop culture, to true Prince followers, *Moments... Remembering Prince* is a must read for all.

— *Donnie Simpson, award-winning radio DJ, TV & movie personality*

Read it cover to cover and never left my chair!! I laughed, I cried. You really brought the memories back crystal clear in a perspective only a close confidant of PRN could do. What fun we had!

— *Matt "Atlanta Bliss" -iii<*

Foreword
by
Eric Leeds

I met Marylou Badeaux in September 1985 at the Warner Bros. Records convention, held at the Diplomat Hotel in Hollywood, Florida. She was there because she was Director of Marketing, Black Music. I was there because… well I'm still not really sure why I was there. I was a member of the group, The Family, which had been formed the previous year by Prince, and our first eponymously named album (on WB of course) had been released in the summer of '85. It yielded a top-ten R&B hit single, "The Screams of Passion". Myself and my band mates (Paul Peterson, Susannah Melvoin, Garry "Jellybean" Johnson, and Jerome Benton) had spent most of the summer rehearsing with our back-up band for a planned fall tour. We had just played our first gig at Minneapolis' famed First Avenue.

But after that gig we were biding our time, waiting for tour plans to come to fruition. Though I lived in Atlanta at the time, I generally bided my time at my parents' condo on the beach in Key Biscayne, Florida, just a few miles down the coast from Hollywood. A close friend of mine, Bob Patton, an independent record promoter, was attending the convention. I had known Bob for years, since his days working with my brother, Alan, for James Brown as a tour director. Anyway, Bob suggested that I hang with him at the convention one evening. So I put on a suit and tie and met him at the Diplomat, figuring I'd glad-hand a few record-company "suits" and have some laughs. (One ALWAYS had laughs with Bob Patton.) Unexpectedly seeing a comrade from the Prince camp, Sheila E. (whose second WB album had just been released) also in attendance, made the evening look more promising.

Even though I had been involved with Prince for over a year and had been performing with his band on the Purple Rain tour, I had no reason to feel that my appearance at the convention would raise any particular interest. Hell, I was only the saxophone player in the group. And I didn't realize that this was the last night of the convention with the final dinner/reception in the main convention hall at the hotel. Before I knew it, I was seated at a table down front with Sheila, Bob, and various execs from "my" record company, including Marylou Badeaux. And before I could stick a fork in the rubber chicken, I was called to the dais to sing the praises of "The Family" and the good fortune that lay ahead for the group and Warner Bros. Records. Marylou later said that her first impression of me, given how I was dressed, was that I looked more like the band's manager than a member of the group. Well, since the group's stage "wardrobe" consisted of pajamas and robes(!), I think everyone had reason to be glad I was wearing a suit that night.

Well, in spite of my grand appearance at the convention, The Family soon after succumbed to fatal familial dysfunction, went kaput(!), and became another in a long list of one-hit wonders. (In 2011 Paul, Susannah, Jellybean and myself reformed the group as "fDeluxe", but that's another story.) I was fortunate enough to land on my feet when Prince asked me to join his band (from The Family into the furnace). And it was as a member of his band that I had the opportunity to become friends with Marylou.

What I learned over time was that Marylou had distinguished herself among her colleagues at WB (and sometimes with their envy) through her unique relationship with Prince. A combination of work ethic, a sense of adventure, and a willingness to appeal to the rule-breaking instincts of the "client" convinced Prince that she was someone he could trust. And because of that, she often joined us on tour for days at a time, organizing all sort of events that in turn appealed to Prince's inherent spontaneity and "thinking outside of the box" instincts. You know, I think there's a book waiting to be written about Marylou's experiences with Prince. Oh, wait a minute, this IS the book about Marylou's experiences with Prince. (Sorry, I forgot that everything I write isn't always supposed to be about myself.)

Marylou soon became part of the tour "family" and we became fast friends, as she did with my brother Alan, my sister-in-law Gwen, and just about everyone else on the tours. By then I was again a WB artist because of the group Madhouse, which had been created by Prince with me as the leader. While it was a funky jazz (or jazzy funk) project, it fell under the purview of the Black Music Department at WB, which meant Marylou would be involved from time to time.

Several years later, after my tenure as a member of Prince's band had ended, Prince signed me to Paisley Park Records (distributed by WB) under my own name (you actually thought I was done writing about myself?). At WB at the time, the Jazz Department was a division of the Black Music Department, so I would have the benefit of Marylou's involvement. By now she was Vice President, Special Projects, Black Music. And around this same time my brother, Alan, had been named by Prince to be the head of Paisley Park Records. Gee, what a wonderful coincidence. Not exactly a bad thing to have your brother running the record company you're signed to. And because of the close friendship that existed between Alan and Marylou, I was in good hands. In fact, Marylou's office at WB headquarters in Burbank, California became the un-official "official" West Coast office of Paisley Park Records. Which meant that whenever Alan had reason to be at WB in Burbank, he would set up shop in Marylou's office. Alan often ran Paisley Park Records from the far corner of the couch in Marylou's office, the one nearest the telephone extension. (This was in the days before cell phones. Proximity to a "land line" was a must.)

While there were several people at WB that always had close ties to Prince and Paisley Park, by now Marylou was THE liaison between WB and anything regarding the Prince organization. Which meant that not only did I have a wonderful friend in my corner, she was a friend that came with a title of Vice President. After my first album was released, I was scheduled to do a promo tour on the East Coast of several WEA offices (WEA was the distribution arm of WB), radio stations, etc. Even though I had the luxury of the "Prince Pedigree", it was easy to get lost in the shuffle among all the projects being released at any given time. But a call by Alan to Marylou resulted in her jumping on a plane and meeting me in Washington, DC to ensure that I received "royal" treatment. Of course, Marylou always enjoyed an excuse to get out of the office for a few days, but a trip like this was generally beneath her pay grade. But she was there not only to support an artist, but more importantly to support a friend. And of course, we always had big fun.

I suppose since the beginning of the recording industry there has always been a natural and often adversarial relationship between the artist and the record company "suits". The artist finds it easy to blame the lack of support by the record company whenever a project is less successful than the artist expected. And the "suits" always found it convenient to suggest that they would have an easier time selling the product if the artist would somehow create something that even remotely resembled something that ordinary people would want to listen to. And like much in life, somewhere in between lies the truth. And Prince was certainly someone who embodied the "artist" perspective when it came to his relationship with WB (or any other record company he was involved with over time). Hell, we all know that for several years he was just that… "THE Artist". (Spoiler Alert… so what the hell do you actually think much of this book is going to be about?) But I bring this up because I had the wonderful opportunity to know a "suit" in the record business that defied all the clichés as to how a record company executive often related to an artist. Speaking as a recording artist, if every record company "suit" was as cool as Marylou, the relationship between artist and record company would be really COOL indeed. But don't just take my word for it. Prince, in his infinite wisdom, offered the same sentiment about Marylou to me one day. And that's coming from "THE Artist"!

So, now excuse me while I finally get out of the way and let Marylou tell her side of the story. It's going to be very cool.

Eric Leeds

June 2017

CONTENTS

Prologue: The Question of WHY?

I struggled for some time about whether I should put these memories down on paper. A lot of information has been published about Prince, and the market has seen much more since his untimely death.

At the urging of a close friend I started writing down some of the moments in time that stay with me.

As memories came flooding back, I realized that I had some rather unique interactions with Prince as well as with the people at Paisley Park. Many of these interactions showed a different side of Prince that no one except those closest to him would even realize existed.

While certainly different from most of us mere mortals, Prince could be as down-to-earth as anyone. He certainly had a sense of humour, easily shown when only those he knew well were in the room.

Yes, being a perfectionist and having whatever "demons" existed from his childhood (documented in many different books) made him a challenge to work around. I always had great respect for those who worked for and with him day to day, as it would have been difficult and challenging but oh so rewarding.

He did not suffer fools and tolerated no one or nothing that reached less than the highest level of excellence (nothing less than he expected of himself).

But there were those moments when that shy, funny, insecure kid came through. There were the times when Prince showed how much he cared, the times he appreciated others even as he struggled with how different he was while living in a world where he was such a unique individual.

I hope some of these moments help give you a different sort of insight into this most extraordinary musician and individual.

Preface: Pop Life
How Did I Get SO Lucky?

So how did a girl from a Boston Irish family end up working with brilliant artists, including Prince?

I was exposed to amazing music from the time I was a young child. My mother played Motown music all day, and my Dad, who loved jazz and big bands, often took me to the renowned Boston jazz club, Storyville. There I was privileged to see artists such as Billie Holiday, Ella Fitzgerald, Johnny Mathis, Louis Armstrong, and so many other amazing artists. I will never forget that at about age eight I was invited to sit on Duke Ellington's lap onstage. What amazing experiences!

With my love for music, I began dancing at the age of four, convinced I could turn professional. As hard as I tried, I just didn't have the talent to make it. My alternate plan was to try to work "behind the scenes". My first job was pure luck. As I sat in the lobby in the #1 radio station in the country at the time, 93 KHJ, the secretary to the Program Director was fired. Right time, right place! I was hired on the spot.

Following that, stints in local television, radio, and finally Warner Bros. Television and Warner Bros. Pictures in assistant roles started filling my resume. However, I MISSED the music! It took me about two years to manage to move over to Warner Bros. Records where I yearned to be.

The Black Music Department was fairly new, and Tom Draper was the recently appointed Vice President, Black Music. He and I hit it off immediately, and he took a HUGE chance on hiring me as his assistant. I imagine he took a lot of criticism from his peers for bringing on a white woman in a job that a black person could easily handle. I am forever grateful to him for his leap of faith. My career was, in large part, due to him as well as a company that loved to give its people the chance to grow and shine. Starting out as an assistant, I held many titles through the years, finding my niche putting together alternative marketing ideas and television specials. After years as the Vice President, Special Projects, Black Music, I finished out my Warner Bros. years as a Vice President in the Jazz Department working with some of the finest jazz musicians around.

Year after year, Warner Bros. Black Music was the #1 black label in the industry (as voted by *Billboard* magazine). We had an amazing roster of artists, which included artists from the P-Funk crew and George Clinton; Chaka Khan, the Curtom group with legendary artist Curtis Mayfield; Earth, Wind & Fire; Ashford & Simpson; George Benson; Al Jarreau; Ice-T; and Larry Graham to the timeless producer and artist Quincy Jones. There were so many others who would take pages to name. My apologies to the many talented artists not named here.

But these memories are about one particular and rather special artist by the name of Prince. Warner Bros. signed him in 1978. And as time passed, we reaped the benefits of his unique ability in finding new talents and nurturing artists already out there. Included in that roster were Sheila E, The Time, Vanity 6, Madhouse, The Family, and others.

Prince was just a very different artist from Day One, and for whatever reason, he and I seemed to "understand" one another. I was extremely fortunate to be at Warner Bros. when we signed Prince. Through many years ending in the mid-nineties, I worked closely with him and the talented people at Paisley Park and made many lifelong friends.

What follows is a bit of a look at some of the moments I shared with Prince and the people around him.

First Encounter of a Different Kind

The Prince signing was exciting for all, as it personified what Warner Bros. was all about. It was never a company to play "safe" with the usual pop signings, instead being open to diverse and unique music.

While Prince was sought after by other record companies as well, the executives at Warner Bros. were the only ones to promise him the freedom he demanded in how he produced and recorded his music. He was also absolute in his vision of not being seen as a "black" artist, but one who could conquer multiple genres. Warner Bros. was the company that shared his vision. It was a unique company for artists and executives alike. This artist-friendly environment was the single biggest factor, in my opinion, that made so many artists feel Warner Bros. was *the* place to be. Frankly, the same creative spirit for executives was why it was considered the epitome of record companies to work for.

A few days after the "official signing", Prince came into the building for what I assumed were meetings with the Chairman, Mo Ostin, and other key executives. As the years rolled on, Prince would often come into the building, silently going up the front stairs directly to Mo or Lenny's (Waronker) office for meetings followed only by his bodyguard. Whispers would ripple through the building: "Prince is here." People would "casually" walk back and forth through the lobby hoping to get a glimpse of him when he left. He had that kind of aura.

I was working in my office when I sensed a presence standing there. I looked up and there was Prince just staring at me. His ability to stare at someone silently was always unnerving. Not knowing what to say, I simply uttered, "Hi, I'm Marylou." Prince answered, "I know who you are." Okay, he's already scoped everyone out. It's something I would learn as time went on that he was uncanny at doing. And, he had a mind like a steel trap.

After he made his comment, he turned without another word and then walked out of my office and straight out the front door of the building.

Hmmm. This is going to be interesting!

Me with the young Prince – 1979

Baby, I'm Gonna Be a Star

Prior to Prince's first "open" showcase in Los Angeles at the Roxy in November 1979, he and the band that he had assembled performed a showcase night at Leeds Instrument Rentals. This evening was strictly for executives at Warner Bros. Records and key media people.

I don't claim to have "A&R ears" at all. (A&R is the "Artist and Repertoire" department, which is mainly staffed by producers and musician types who have an ability to hear talent before it's developed. It's the department that usually signs new acts.) At this point in his career, Prince was not polished or used to being in front of crowds, and the band was new.

I was, of course, quite excited to see Prince at this point to see what all the talk was about. I was also quite curious after our unusual encounter in my office. Little did I know at that point that he and his organization would become so integral to many projects I worked on in the future, to my very career, and most importantly, to future and lifelong friendships.

I invited a couple of colleagues from the music trade magazines to join me, as I wanted them to be excited about this new signing.

Of course, the showcase performance was rough. Of course,

he had a long way to go, but even without the ability to hear talent in the rough stages, I just knew I was witnessing something incredibly special. The two gentlemen I took with me agreed.

Look out world. Baby, he IS gonna be a star!

The Roxy Theatre in West Hollywood was the site of Prince's first public showcase, and it has a fascinating history. Go to: http://www.theroxy.com/ to learn more about this famous venue.

Men are from Mars, Prince is from Pluto

Yes, artists are different. Yes, they "march to a different drummer" – some more so than others.

Then there's Prince. I suspect that no one has ever gotten inside his head and figured him out. He was just VERY different. I often got the feeling that he saw everyone around him moving in slow motion, as he was living on a different plane than normal folks. The term "whirling dervish" comes to mind!

He definitely wasn't up for the typical promotional activities that most artists would partake in – if not happily, at least grudgingly to advance their careers. Artists understood, and continue to understand, the benefits and need to "get out there". Some actually quite enjoy that aspect of their careers and use it to greatly benefit their visibility.

After the release of his second album, *PRINCE*, I took him to a magazine for a major interview. We considered this a very important step in exposing him to the people who would buy his records. It was clear from the moment I picked Prince up that he did not feel the same. He remained completely silent on the way, even though I tried to give him a bit of background on the magazine and the interviewer. He was somewhere else entirely.

The interviewer, taken slightly aback by Prince's shortage of clothing, got right into it by asking, "where are you from". BIG mistake! Anyone who had read Prince's bio knew the answer and that this would not endear the interviewer to Prince in any way. Of course, the interviewer was probably just trying to break the ice.

In a way only he could deliver in that surprisingly deep voice of his, Prince answered, "Pluto". This stunned the interviewer into silence. I suspect that's exactly what Prince counted on. He then proceeded to tell the person all about the trip to Earth. He was so serious in his delivery that I was laughing like crazy (on the inside... I didn't dare even crack a smile).

Without stopping, Prince turned the tables and started interviewing the interviewer, asking some pretty personal questions that I won't repeat. It was clear this interview was not a good idea and I had to get us out of there FAST. So many years later, I'm not sure exactly what I said, but we were up and out. On the way downstairs I asked him why he said what he said and then followed up with inappropriate questions.

As I suspected, he hated what he felt were "stupid" questions (even though just an icebreaker from the interviewer). He wanted nothing to do with interviews and the "normal" way of promoting. Even then, just 18, he was declaring, "anyone who really LISTENS to my music doesn't have to ask questions. It's all there." "Besides," he added, "you thought it was funny too." What, so now he can get into my head? I would learn he was very good at that as well.

Okay, throw out the promotion handbook. Little did I know at that point how much he would rewrite the way things had conventionally been done in the music business.

No wonder, many years later, he would lead the charge on artists' rights vis-à-vis record labels (another very sticky wicket for which there are very legitimate arguments on both sides).

Let's Go Crazy

Warner Bros. Records was known for being "artist-friendly". The company would stick by an artist, album after album, until the artist reached his or her potential (something that really doesn't exist in the industry today for many different reasons).

Prince was the perfect example of an artist the record company had complete faith in, and the company was determined to help him reach the heights everyone believed he could reach.

From very early on, not only was the R&B promotion department working extremely hard, with some terrific results, but the pop department was determined to "cross him over" into the pop world.*

The album *1999* was the first the pop department had success with. Interestingly, the main reason was that Prince's next album was a long time coming (in the world of Prince), as he was busy filming a little movie by the name of *Purple Rain*. The R&B department had already had massive success with *1999*, and with the gap in albums, the pop department had the time to revisit singles from 1999 and "break" Prince at the pop level.

The stage was set as the Purple Rain album was released in June 1984 and the movie followed in July. All of a sudden EVERYONE wanted/needed to see Prince in concert.

Overnight, he was a superstar. While it was amazing to be involved, the whirlwind was enough to knock everyone down.

I attended the world premiere of the movie at the famous Grauman's Chinese Theatre (temporarily renamed as Mann's Chinese Theatre from 1973 to 2001) in Hollywood, where the crowds screamed and lined the streets waiting for a glimpse of Prince (and the band). The feeling of anticipation inside the theatre was palpable. And, keep in mind this was your typical Hollywood premiere with many industry types who don't get excited about too many things. The premiere was followed by a star-studded after-party at the Palace nightclub.

Who could have known that the platform was set for the tsunami to come. Perhaps Prince knew as he sang, "on the 4th day of November, we will reach a purple high" (lyrics from "All the Critics Love U in New York", a cut on the *1999* album, which gave us a hint.... The huge PURPLE RAIN Tour opened in Detroit on the 4th day of November in 1984).

I attended that momentous event, taking a couple of magazine writers with me. A large number of us went out for dinner first, and I noticed that EVERYONE in the restaurant was wearing purple! That couldn't be a coincidence. We were witnessing history being made.

The moment I will never forget as the lights went down:

Dearly beloved
We are gathered here today...

The roar of the crowd never stopped from that point. Goosebump time!

And so, suddenly everyone involved (both at the record company and Paisley Park) was in the middle of the tsunami with him. Requests for tickets (demands from some) were insane. For the first time, we were faced with "competition" between R&B radio and pop radio for ticket access, as well as where the seats were in the venues. A representative from the pop department and I worked tirelessly trying to keep things "fair". I have memories of us sitting at a large table with the physical tickets and a map of each venue in front of us, attempting to keep the allocation as balanced as possible. As hard as we tried, it was never enough.

Meanwhile out on tour, it had turned into a circus. It's the old story of EVERYONE wanting to be part of something so big. There were people everywhere, all craving to be close to this phenomenon. I'm sure it was a challenge for the key tour people and crew! I made the decision to stay away from backstage during the tour. It was just

TOO crazy!

Of course, I was thrilled for Prince, the Revolution, and everyone involved that the world was finally embracing this tremendous talent.

* In the world of radio, it can be extraordinarily frustrating because artists are labeled irrespective of the genre of music they create. A black artist is considered to "belong" at R&B radio. This of course was one of the key reasons Prince signed with Warner Bros., as a commitment was made that the record company would NOT pigeonhole him into the R&B department. Of course, the challenge is to get radio to understand that this is an artist who just happens to be black but plays rock and roll, jazz, R&B, etc. It's a conundrum that has plagued the industry for a very long time.

In fact, MTV didn't play ANY black artists' videos until Michael Jackson's "Billie Jean". And just because they played that video did not mean that it became any easier for black artists at the network. It was always a struggle whenever we had a "crossover" (crossing from R&B to pop airplay) artist, be it Prince or any of our other artists who crossed genres. That's a subject for an entirely different book!

Around the World with Prince

Artists would at times come into the building at Warner Bros. to have a listening session for a new album. Sometimes the listening sessions were set up at a recording studio.

While most listening sessions were straight-ahead and predictable, anything involving Prince took on a different approach. With very little notice (he was VERY good at that concept), a small "event" was put together for the conference room where invited execs could hear his highly anticipated "follow-up" album to the massive *Purple Rain*.

Anyone who knew Prince knew that the album wouldn't be the traditional follow-up but a complete 180-degree turn in another direction.* "Follow-up" albums simply weren't in his vocabulary. Done with one thing, he'd move on. I got the sense that most of the Warner Bros. execs felt the next album would take advantage of the roll he had started (I should probably refer to it as an avalanche) with the groundbreaking *Purple Rain* album. Of course, that also would have been wishful thinking on their part.

I just knew (as I'm sure others in the room must have realized) that the album he'd play for us would be something vastly different from *Purple Rain*. It was just a question of what he'd come up with.

His instructions had been clear: dim the lights and close the drapes. Everyone should be seated on one of the chairs placed around the edge of the vast room or on the floor. The huge conference table had been removed, so there was no sense of this being a "cold conference room".

Everyone was there, anticipating his arrival. He walked in with Wendy and Lisa, who threw flower petals on the floor.

I remember thinking that they were dressed as if their next stop was a pajama party, as they were all in lovely silk pajama-type clothes.

Lights down. Prince, Wendy and Lisa all sat cross-legged in the middle of the floor. I was on the floor, not far from him, when he looked over and nodded.

As typical, Prince had nothing to say. After all, the music always spoke for him. We were about to hear "Around the World in a Day". The first notes struck and there was a shifting in the room. Suddenly we were thrust into the world of Middle Eastern music, which is a tough sell at pop radio. I could see some of the promotion execs with perplexed looks on their faces. This definitely wasn't "Purple Rain 2". Didn't they realize that mountain had been climbed and conquered and it was time to move on? He was NEVER going to do the predictable, and this was no exception. While he wanted success at radio, he was never going to record "formula" music.

As the music continued, the mood continued to shift from one cut to the next. I did not glance his way at all. I suspected he wasn't overly happy with the reactions in the room. As the album came to a close, Prince, Wendy and Lisa all got up and quickly left the room. Not a word was spoken, no eye contact with anyone.

It was clear that this next project was going to be a challenge for everyone!

* In many ways, this really wasn't a "follow-up" album as it had been recorded during the *Purple Rain* tour. But, I'll leave those sorts of details to the writers who have thoroughly covered the recording end of his career.

20

Have I Fallen Down the Rabbit Hole?

MTV came up with what was thought to be a brilliant promotion for the debut of the *Under the Cherry Moon* movie and the *Parade* soundtrack. The winner would have a date with Prince, attending the premiere in their hometown. Of course, they'd be able to invite many of their friends along. What more exciting opportunity than the chance to go on a "date" with the one and only PRINCE? Definitely a dream come true for some lucky fan!

Naturally, everyone figured that the winner would hail from a big city like New York, Chicago, Cleveland, Los Angeles, etc. There'd be the chance for major press coverage, limousines, an MTV special and all the trappings with minimal effort.

Drum Roll...

The winner was the 10,000th caller on MTV live. And the winner was...

Lisa Barber from Sheridan, Wyoming. Huh? Where and what is Sheridan, Wyoming? How do we get there? How does MTV get all their equipment there to cover the premiere and after-party? Where does Prince PERFORM his after-party in a small town? How about details like limos, catering, the theatre itself? YIKES, it's a logistical nightmare that MTV and Warner Bros. Pictures will have to work out, with a big pitch-in by the wizards up at Paisley Park.

Warner Bros. Pictures, the Paisley people and MTV folks went into high gear to make it happen. I was getting updates on everything from where everyone would stay (the Holiday Inn Sheridan), where the limos were coming from (you wouldn't believe the logistics on that one), how to transport the guests, band and MTV crew there (fly to Denver and then a "puddle-jumper" to Sheridan) and more. The problem of where to have the performance/after-party was critical due to technical requirements, both for the band itself and for MTV to beam it live on TV. Fortunately, the Holiday Inn did have a ballroom, albeit a small one. One big problem was the ceiling height. By the time you put the stage in, the band was almost touching the ceiling. And of course that made the stage an incredibly hot place to perform. This conference room was built for conferences, not a performance by a rock star. And with that, we are not even addressing the acoustic issues!

It was a couple of days until the big event. I was in Burbank getting the blow-by-blow. All was good until I received a call from Minneapolis. If they were heading out on this adventure, so was I, so I'd better get on a plane pronto. Okay, but all flights from Denver to Sheridan (not many, I can assure you) were completely booked. I thought I'd gotten out of going but NO. Up at Paisley Park, they were busy finding an alternative way for me to get there.

And so, my adventure began. First, a flight from Los Angeles to Salt Lake City. Change planes and head to Billings, Montana! I would then be driven from Billings to Sheridan, Wyoming (about 140 miles) by a local volunteer. One thing that had been done was to enlist the help of several locals (college students, etc.) to help with various errands and chores that needed to be done. Volunteers were EVERYWHERE. Everyone wanted to be part of what would be the BIGGEST event to ever hit their small town.

As soon as I landed in Billings, I knew I had entered an alternative universe from what I was accustomed to. As I walked through the small terminal, I had several opportunities to buy handcrafted moccasins and beautiful Indian blankets.

Waiting at curbside was a lovely young lady named Lynda. She had a homemade sign with my name, and she was dressed in her best western wear, boots, and Stetson and driving a really big station wagon. I got into the front seat and off we went. She was so excited by the entire experience that she never stopped talking about the town and the people.

Custer's Last Stand

All was good until, in the middle of nowhere, Lynda pulled over to the side. A bit concerned (I had NO idea where we were), I asked why we had stopped as the car seemed to be running just fine and I noted there was plenty of gas. She then happily told me she wanted me to experience Custer's Last Stand at Little Big Horn. Okayyy. All I know is that we were pulled off on the side of a highway with nothing in sight in any direction. She told me to be patient. A few more minutes passed and, over the hill to one side, here came the Indians on horseback. In the far distance, I could see Custer's men. I had definitely entered the Twilight Zone as I watched a reenactment of that famous battle. If I had taken the time to look at a map before getting on the plane, I would have discovered that we would be driving straight through Little Big Horn National Park! We were simply viewing it from the "back" side.

With Custer losing yet again, we headed off. As we pulled away, I noted bleachers in the far distance where people could view the reenactment inside the park. Phew. I wasn't hallucinating.

When we reached the town of Sheridan, Lynda wanted to drive me around town. I certainly felt I owed her that, so we toured the town, which took under five minutes. There were Prince signs in every window and guys dressed up like the cowboys in the movies perched in various pickup trucks along Main Street. It was like the Fourth of July! They were all in a very celebratory mood.

The one thing that kept crossing my mind was that these townfolk didn't appear to be what I would classify as Prince "fans". They looked like heavy-duty rock dudes and dudettes. Oh well, better not profile!

Time to get to the hotel and find the Paisley people so I can tell them about my adventurous trip in.

Never a dull moment around Prince and his people! This definitely was not going to be an ordinary couple of days. But what was I thinking? It's NEVER ordinary around Prince.

Downtown Sheridan, Wyoming!

Holiday Inn – Sheridan
Never the same after the 1st of July, 1986

I opted against attending the premiere itself and made myself busy in the ballroom for anything the crew might need before the after-show.

Prior to the movie, there was a parade down Main Street where all the locals lined the street. Prince picked up his date by jumping over her front fence. He seemed to be in great spirits and

YOU ARE CORDIALLY INVITED TO THE
GALA PREMIERE PARTY OF

PRINCE
Under the
CHERRY MOON

Dress casual Black & White
July 1, 1986
8:30 PM
Immediately Following Screening
HOLIDAY INN
Sheraton Convention Center

ADMIT ONE

determined to make the experience memorable for everyone.

The buzz in the ballroom was intense as locals, MTV folks, and celebs filled the room in anticipation of a live performance. Prince did not disappoint (he NEVER disappointed in live performances, as he was an amazing performer on every level). I really felt sorry for the band, in full costume (of course), with that low ceiling and the temperature soaring under the lights. I stood to the side below the stage with Billy Sparks, and we were both sweating something awful.

Prince performed six songs and the entire audience was

delir~~ious~~ ~~happy.~~

Setlist
Prince
Parade Tour
Holiday Inn, Sheridan, WY, USA
July 1, 1986

Raspberry Beret
Delirious
Controversy
Mutiny (The Family cover)
Do Me, Baby
Purple Rain

The show was over, but the buzz continued. Members of the band came out and mingled, much to the delight of the locals. Meanwhile, I discovered that I had a VERY unhappy winner from a contest I had run on BET (Black Entertainment Television). The young lady, who won a trip to Sheridan to attend both the premiere and the after-show, arrived AFTER the show due to a cancelled flight. She was distraught. Trying to make her feel a bit better, I grabbed Wendy and Lisa, quickly explaining the situation to them. They were terrific and spent a few minutes with the winner, who had now stopped crying.

Out of the corner of my eye, I saw that Prince was standing in a hallway, perhaps deciding if he would come out and "mingle" or retreat to his room. I decided to go over and tell him what had happened, just in case. After I quickly told him about her disappointment, he asked me to bring her over. YEAH!!! I didn't tell her where I was taking her. When she saw who was there, smiling at her, she almost lost it. Prince said, "I understand you missed the movie and the show". In a meek voice, she answered, "Yes". He asked if she'd like a picture taken with him. OMG!!! Shaking, she gave me her camera and I quickly took a couple of pictures. He smiled and vanished like a puff of smoke, as he was known to do. I had trouble peeling her off the ceiling she was sailing so high. A disaster had been made into the greatest experience she could have hoped for! This situation alone had made the trip to Sheridan worthwhile and a good lesson for anyone in my position. ALWAYS make certain there is someone there from the record company to intercede in case something goes wrong. I would often weigh up spending company money on trips, not wanting to be wasteful or take advantage. Sometimes that can be taken too far. Once again, my friends at Paisley had me in the right place at the right time!

I was as happy as I could possibly be and decided it was time to get back to my room and get my sweat-drenched clothes off. I entered the elevator and two young men came running in as the door closed. Next thing you know they were pitching a song to me, singing, trying to hand me a cassette. "But we saw you with the band. We saw you with Prince. Surely you can help get this cassette to him?" Imagine if you worked directly for a major star and this happened to you all the time? Yikes!

(Note: There is a good wrap-up of the event in the *Los Angeles Times:* http://articles.latimes.com/1986-07-03/entertainment/ca-1181_1_warner-bros.)

Wild Wild West

It was the morning after the big event at the Holiday Inn. I walked down the road to pick up the newspaper. Completely sold out. With Prince on the front page and a blow-by-blow account of the day, there wasn't a paper to be had anywhere in town.

So the adventure was over, or so I thought. Because my air reservations had been made so late, the only flight I could get was leaving much later in the day. I didn't have a clue on how I would fill the day until I got a phone call in my room.

Those of us "left behind" had been invited to spend the day at someone's ranch. That sounded like a good way to pass a few hours. I was left with about five of the MTV people and one of the film's actresses. A van was provided to take us to this ranch.

It turned out this wasn't just ANY ranch. It belonged to someone with BIG money. Once we passed through the gate, we drove for a couple more miles until a huge home appeared in front of us. As we got out of the van, we were greeted by the ranch owner and his wife. They were extremely gracious as they offered us a choice of relaxing by the pool, horseback riding, hiking, drinks in the bar, and food set up in various places. Most of us decided it was time to head to the bar and discovered one of the largest rooms I've seen in a private home. There was a huge bar and, believe it or not, all of the ten or twelve bar stools were saddles!

The maids (yes, plural) started bringing out a huge selection of food, and we all settled down for what we decided would be a terrific day.

In our tour of the home, the actress decided the en-suite bath was where she would spend the day, soaking in a massive spa while watching a television that was built into the wall (remember that this was before flat-screens). We didn't see her again until we left.

After the frenzy of the last few days, we all enjoyed our time relaxing and hearing about the cattle ranch nestled up against the picturesque Rocky Mountains.

All of a sudden, a man came roaring into the house screaming that we had to leave PRONTO if we were to make our plane as it was leaving early! This fellow turned out to be the sheriff. Reluctantly, we all piled back into the van. What happened next had to be witnessed to be believed.

The sheriff drove a classic PURPLE Cadillac! Yes, I was definitely still down the rabbit hole. I knew no one would believe me, so I managed to get a picture before we headed off. He led us, at

breakneck speed, back down the highway to the airport. Within moments we heard gunshots. Okay, I had already witnessed "Custer's Last Stand". Were we under attack again? I looked out and the sheriff had his arm out the window shooting into the air! Yep, it was definitely Twilight Zone time.

We were a bit late for the plane, but of course the sheriff got them to hold it for us. We squeezed into the puddle jumper that held about twelve passengers and were served a paper cup of five M&Ms each (they must be rationed in Wyoming). On our way to Denver, we landed several times, delivering and picking up mail, milk (hence the name "milk run"?), and other miscellaneous items from the local ranches. It was only about 400 miles to Denver, but it took over four hours to get there (a flight that is listed as one hour and twenty minutes)!

By the time we reached Denver, we were sore from laughing! Of course, we missed our Denver connections to Los Angeles and New York. Everyone groaned, but I had the answer: Let's head to the bar! Several hours later, laughing our heads off about our experience, we somehow made our way to our flights back home and reality.

Time to climb back out of the rabbit hole!

All the Critics Love You in New York...
and Chicago... and Los Angeles

There was tremendous disappointment that the SIGN "O" THE

TIMES concert tour was not coming to America. There were great

songs on the double-album, and of course Prince fans could NEVER

get enough of him in concert!

Instead of the tour, Prince put together a concert movie with additional footage shot at his Paisley Park facility in Chanhassen, Minnesota. The movie would be the next best thing for the faithful.

So many years later I don't remember the details, but somehow I got voted by my Paisley friends to welcome fans at the special radio-sponsored premieres in New York, Chicago, and Los Angeles. Sounds easy, right? Well, it's the proverbial "gotta be in three places at once".

I started out in New York and did the introduction. WOW – entrusted with opening up each of the screenings with a few words! What was racing through my mind at that point was, "Thank goodness I took that speech class in college".

As soon as I finished, I raced to the airport and headed to Chicago, barely making it. After the intro, once again I was off, this time to Los Angeles. The only thing that worked in my favour was that I continued to gain time as I flew west. For at least one of the screenings, Sheila E joined me, which, in my opinion, made much more sense. After all, she was a Paisley artist, well recognized, and therefore the perfect person to put in front of the audiences.

I didn't even get to see the movie at that point. I finally sat down a week later to enjoy it.

And you thought being in the music biz was nothing but The Glamorous Life.

Why You Wanna Treat Him So Bad?

Prince decided to organize another new album listening session, this time for *Lovesexy*. As was the case three years earlier with *Around the World in a Day*, organizing his wish to play the record for Warner Bros. execs came together quickly. (I'm not sure he ever comprehended the concept of planning in advance. If he woke up wanting to do a listening session or shoot a video, or anything else, he expected those around him to facilitate it.) And so, once again the huge conference table was removed from the main conference room.

On this occasion, Prince arrived with Joni Mitchell, an artist for whom he had tremendous respect.

By now, I think it was clear to everyone that you could have no pre-conceptions of what the album might sound like and how many "hits" (meaning radio-friendly cuts) were on the record.

As the album unfolded, it was clear that it was a bit more "accessible". As he "vibed" the room it appeared that he felt the execs reacted more to his liking. *

In fact, he stayed on when the music was done to have a bit of a chat with some of those attending. That was another clear sign he was happy, as he was not one to just hang around.

All seemed to be going well until he looked over my way and gave me a look that I interpreted as "get over here". I walked over casually and tuned in on the conversation he was having with one of the execs. I noted that he was doing all the listening and this exec was glancing at a small notebook, as he had made notes during the playing of the album.

Sure enough, the exec was going over the album, cut by cut, making suggestions to change or "tweak" it. "Oh no," I thought. Not only was it not the right forum (several execs milling about) to tell Prince to make changes in his music, you just didn't tell Prince how to compose and/or construct his music. At this point, Prince was glaring at me as if to say, "fix it". I really couldn't, which I tried to relate back by my look to him.

Prince's answer was simple. He spun on his high heels and strode out without another word.

He never brought it up to me, but based on observations on my part, it was clear he made certain that he would never be anywhere near this particular person again.

* Prince, in my opinion, was always someone who had a strong "sixth sense" in reading people, as I had seen it in action time and time again. Some people just have an ability to read people's mood and body language much more easily than others. We probably all have the ability, but some of us have fine-tuned that sixth sense. I do know he could read an audience immediately, and the way he delivered a show could quickly "switch up" to fit it – perhaps funkier or more rock delivered. He gave the folks what they wanted while never compromising.

Glamorous Life

Did I mention how incredibly wonderful the people around Prince were? I made lifelong friends with so many, whether it was band members, Paisley personnel, tour people, hair, makeup, wardrobe – you name it! I stay in touch with many to this day. There was a certain solace in that circle as we reached out to one another when Prince died. The only reason I don't name names is that I don't want to leave anyone out.

So, this time it was a phone call from Paisley to come join them in London for the LOVESEXY Tour. I was going through some challenging personal issues and they all felt that I needed a break, some wonderful music and great friends.

They didn't need to ask twice. I was on a plane immediately! From the moment I reached the lobby of the Mayfair Hotel, it was clear that I was in for a terrific time.

One friend grabbed me for a night to see *Phantom of the Opera* on London's West End, and a group of us went out for dinner at a Japanese restaurant. I had never tasted Sake before and quite enjoyed a few, not realizing how potent the drink is.

The next day found me at a record store in Piccadilly Circus with Prince and the band as they did an autograph session. It was pandemonium! It was extremely rare for him to do an in-store appearance, and it was easy to see why. It's very hard to control the crowd!

As the band sat down at a long table to sign records and tour books, I stood to the side. Suddenly, the Sake was letting me know that I had drunk way too much of it the night before. I began having sweats and feeling green while trying to focus on the signing. The next thing I knew I was frantically looking for a wastebasket... no description needed. I've never touched Sake since.

Gett Off... Please!

Okay, I finally felt a bit steadier, and it was time to leave the signing, get into the cars and go back to the hotel.

The crush of fans blasted us the moment we hit the sidewalk. I was caught up in it just because of who I was with. I wouldn't wish this life on anyone! Just as I felt myself falling, one of the bodyguards grabbed me and literally threw me into a limo. I was bruised and battered but safe.

Another example of the Glamorous Life!

I Get Delirious

The LOVESEXY American Tour was gearing up in Minneapolis with a planned opening at the Met Center in Bloomington on the 14th of September, 1988.

As was often the case, a big opening night after-party was planned. (In fact, this happened on many artist tours, with closing night parties also common.) Of course, the Prince version of an opening night after-party always became a "BIGGER than Life" event. In this case, it was to be so large that a tent had to be constructed on the property of the Paisley Park Studio!

I flew to Minneapolis to help put the party together, working from an office at the Paisley Park facility that was graciously made available for me. I always enjoyed my time at Paisley Park, as it gave me a chance to see and spend time with the many people there whom I had grown to consider as friends, not just "co-workers".

Everyone who worked at Paisley Park put in very long hours, and during my stay there, I was no different. There was a tremendous amount of organizing to do, and of course constant changes, additions, who's on the list, who isn't on the list, who is flying in from Warner Bros. headquarters in Burbank, etc.

Then, in the evening, I'd head off to dinner with at least one of the folks there, getting back to my hotel room late. As tired as I was, I LOVED each and every one of those social get-togethers, whether it was "behind-the-scenes" people or members of the band.

The day of the show and party was, of course, as hectic as it could be. The phone didn't stop ringing, as all sorts of people called looking for tickets for the show and entry to the after-party. Paisley Park offices fielded most of those calls, while I dealt with last-minute requests from the record label side of things.

I barely made it back to the hotel in time to change and race to the venue.

The show was amazing and of course was received as the incredible evening that it was. This particular tour was "in the round" with all sorts of props, staging and the like. (In fact, due to the extensive staging, in spite of sold-out shows, it didn't go into the black until after the American tour when Prince took it to Japan.)

As the encore was going on, I raced out to the car I had rented and bolted over to Paisley Park, about 15 miles away, to be in place as people started arriving. My adrenalin was pumping. I had just seen a wonderful show, had seen the audience go crazy, and was now readying for the After-Party Show.

This "event after the event" was quite exciting. Naturally, Prince and his band did a set (anyone who has had the privilege to see one of his late night club shows knows how amazing these are). Wendy and Lisa came. George Clinton and Mavis Staples added to the flavour of the evening. The After-Party went for hours, and I never even had a chance to sit down. I finally had the opportunity to get back in the car and head for the hotel and very much wanted bed and sleep.

I didn't realize how exhausted I was until I went out into the car park at the studio. Try as I might, I couldn't figure out which car I was driving. My mind had truly reached a blank. After hitting the alarm button on my remote over and over, I finally found the car and drove to the hotel. To this day, I'm not sure how I drove back to the hotel in one piece.

I crashed in my bed, thinking HOW do the Paisley people and the band manage this kind of lifestyle week in and week out?

The next morning I awoke around 9 a.m. (late for me) and saw the message light blinking. Hmmm... I hadn't heard the phone.

There was a message from Paisley at 8 a.m. "Where are you? We're all at Paisley." Prince was already there and at work!

I was thinking they had to be kidding. I knew I wasn't cut out for that kind of pace! Methinks it was time to head back to Los Angeles!

Paisley Park Studios in the 1980s

This is where the magic happened.

(I took these pictures in the late 1980s on one of my visits.)

The Atrium area was beautifully lit from the pyramid skylights above.
(Note the cage for the doves up on the balcony.)

The ever-changing pictures line the wall of the front staircase.

What Time is It???

Candy Corner

WARDROBE DEPARTMENT

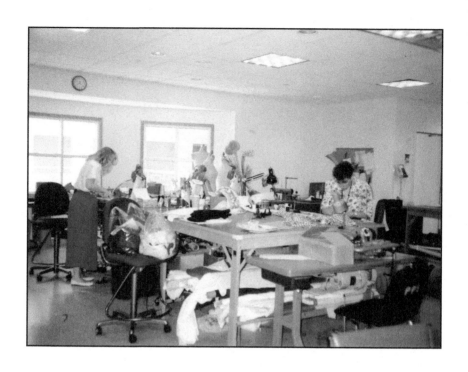

The underground garage was a treasure trove of all things Prince. The photograph below shows a collection of road cases that were dispatched when Prince went out on tour.

Also here are a couple of photographs of just two of his famous motorcycles. This corner of the garage housed several motorcycles!

I definitely could have spent hours exploring this part of the building.

Studio A

The studio where Prince did his recording.
Great pains would go into "setting the mood"
when he actually recorded there.

Just imagine Prince sitting at this piano, creating his music.

This is the anteroom to the famous vault. It is filled with his awards, as well as gold and platinum records. He always loved decorating with veils and scarves, which gave the room an almost "Middle Eastern" feel.

There are awards everywhere in the anteroom. Here are some of his most prized ones, including his Oscar for the PURPLE RAIN soundtrack.

The Famous Vault

Here is the actual vault door. Beyond it are the treasures of Prince's work. While I was privileged to enter the vault, I did not take pictures out of respect.

When not recording, this is the desk he'd work from
in a fully equipped office and sanctuary.

People don't realize how fit an artist must be to handle a grueling
schedule of concert tours. An artist at Prince's level, expending
huge amounts of energy on stage, definitely had to be fit...
and he WAS!

Just in case he wants a bit of a rest…

Technology has moved on just a bit. I'm sure this entertainment area has changed dramatically since the time of this photo in the late 1980s!

Here's a view up to the pyramid window

in Prince's office with its opening to the stars.

Dancing with the Star

Going out on portions of artist tours may sound very glamorous, and compared to a "normal" job it certainly is. Of course, there are the downsides to it as well. Very long hours, losing touch with what city you're in, different hotel rooms almost every night, and a myriad of other challenges. For instance, imagine being out with an artist whose music you don't care for!

That was never the case with Prince. His live shows were different EVERY night as he adjusted for the mood of the audience as well as his own mood. There was always a certain structure to the set list, but the way it was delivered and what might pop up in the middle was always a surprise.

I know as someone who attended night after night, it made for a wonderful experience at every show. You simply never got bored!

During the LOVESEXY Tour, I was on the road with him a fair bit. I felt it important to support him and the band on a tour and album that was not as "popular" a tour as PURPLE RAIN, a tour where everyone and his mama was out there, all trying to get a piece of the action. I believe he and certainly the band appreciated the support.

One of my favorite cuts on the album was "I Wish You Heaven". On tour, it acquired a magical feel as he took it to another and VERY Funky level. Every night, regardless of what I was doing backstage, a couple of the ladies in wardrobe and make-up and I would make our way to the side of the stage (in the round) so we could groove to it. Within days, we had our own routine. Prince noticed us, and from that moment, it was ON! He'd come over and look down at the three of us (wonder what he thought of us three with our own choreography?), and we would feed off each other. He'd play the "you-know-what" out of his guitar giving us one of his grins, and we would answer back with our dancing prowess. No words were ever spoken but he showed up on the side of the stage every night to check us out as he played to an enraptured audience. No one but he (and we) ever knew we were there!

Honey on the Console

There was never a dull moment in the world of Prince. The original *Batman* movie was filming, and Prince was asked to write some music for it.

Visiting the set in the UK, he met the various cast members. It's common knowledge that he and Kim Basinger definitely hit it off.

While I did not witness this myself, there were lots of "inside stories" going around about the recording of the sexy song, "Scandalous", as Kim was in the studio with him.

I heard everything from "honey on the console" to… Well, I'll leave it there.

Working in promotion at the record company, I was always thinking about clever ways to promote our records. We were always looking for that little "something" that made a record stand out when our promotion gurus delivered the records into the radio stations looking for an add to the playlist.

Regardless of what may or may not have happened during the actual recording, the stories got me to thinking. How about little jars of "Scandalous" honey to go with the record delivery? After all, honey is known as something that can be quite sexy. And with Prince's sense of humour, I could see this as a clever gimmick.

The jars went over big time and quickly became collector's

items. And you can imagine all the stories those little jars started!

Alan Leeds, Vice President at Paisley Park, and I on the Batdance video set on the Warner Bros. Studio lot

The Lovesexy Tour

On the Road with Billy Sparks and Alan Leeds

King vs. Prince

I was out on a portion of the LOVESEXY American Tour, and we had reached the venerable Blues city of Memphis, Tennessee.

As it happened, we had a day off. Some chose to simply "chill" for the day, as it was a rare time when one could sleep and get recharged.

Others, itching to get out of the hotel, decided to make a pilgrimage to Graceland, the home of Elvis Presley.

That sounded like a great idea to me! We asked if we could use one of the tour vans, and several of us headed off to this famous Memphis landmark. Some of the band came along as well as wardrobe, make-up, and other miscellaneous tour personnel. The mood was light and we were off.

As soon as you get close to the home, the souvenir stands, tacky cafes, etc., surround you. We had to laugh. Okay, time to get serious and soak in the ambiance of Graceland itself.

We continued to joke our way through a home with, shall we say, "interesting" décor. A couple of the wise guys in the band kept the humour going.

We reached the museum of Elvis's costumes. I noted that the people from Prince's wardrobe department made sure they had a good look at the various outfits. More giggling as someone noted how "large" the outfits were towards the end of his life (okay, so we showed very little decorum – we were having fun).

As we left, someone suggested we head over to one of the tacky souvenir stores. That was the beginning of the end. We all scooped up ridiculous tchotchkes, from a bobbing head of Elvis to toilet paper (and holder of course), plates, cups, and other sundry items, not sure what we would ever do with them. It just seemed a good idea at the time and everyone was laughing their heads off.

The next night backstage at the venue someone had collected all these ridiculous items and set up a shrine to Elvis Presley! If only I had a camera at the time (this was before mobile phones with cameras – yes, there was such a time) to document this special corner dedicated to the King.

With giggling in the background, Prince walked past and took a sidelong glance without stopping. He had a hard time not showing one of his grins as he just shook his head and kept walking.

Mission accomplished. The shrine was quickly disassembled for complete deniability.

What shrine?

Cocooning

Being "on the road" as crew and tour personnel may sound like loads of fun but can also be very stressful. Different tours, of course, support various numbers of behind-the-scenes people. In Prince's case, it was always a large number who bonded due to length of time on tour and the fact that the tour members did so much together, both within the tour structure and on days off.

But imagine living out of suitcases, perhaps months at a time, working very long hours with only an occasional day off. Great way to see the world, you might say. Most cities are seen from the windows of the buses.

Overall, I found Prince didn't mix much with the personnel while on tour. It just wasn't his style to "hang out". But one thing he did do was organize the hiring of a movie theatre in various cities when there were multiple days in one place. Being Prince, he wouldn't have these movies shown during the day. Instead, the movie would have a showing around 2:30 in the morning, AFTER the gig! It helps that most musicians are, by their very nature, night people. If you work around them, you have to adjust! Of course, if the show was in the same venue the next night, you probably didn't have to go to work until around two or three in the afternoon. If, on the other hand, you were heading to the next city, the teardown of the set would happen directly after the show and the trucks would head off in the middle of the night as soon as they were loaded. Key support personnel (hair, make-up, tour manager, and other key people) and the band would catch a plane the next morning, often with an early lobby call (the time everyone had to be in the hotel lobby and ready to leave).

We were somewhere in the American South on the LOVESEXY Tour. Word came down after the gig finished that there would be a movie playing at that magic hour of 2:30 a.m. in a small theatre Prince had rented for everyone. I learned that the snack bar would be open for anything we wanted, included! The movie to be shown was *Cocoon*, the heartwarming film starring such greats as Don Ameche and Hume Cronyn. I figured, "why not"! A couple of vans were provided and we were off. I was thinking that I must be out of my mind. I had to get up early, as I had other responsibilities which had to be handled from the phone in my hotel room during normal business hours. And, I never was a "night person". Oh well.

We all got our big bags of popcorn and sat back to enjoy the film. I did everything I could to stay awake.

Behind me, two rows back, were two of Prince's current "lady interests". I noted they sat together with an open seat between them, apparently reserved for Prince. I must say that observing the interaction between them was almost as interesting as watching the movie! My imagination was going crazy thinking about what would happen if/when Prince plopped down between them. Perhaps they were hoping for a bit of their own cocooning?

Well, Prince did show up and sat two rows BEHIND his lady friends. He sat by himself, watching the movie for about 20 minutes. I looked back and he had slipped out – probably to head back into the studio with more music swirling in his head. I must say that I found the whole interaction (and "non-interaction") fun and fascinating to watch. And the movie was pretty good too!

Look, Don't Look

I was invited to visit the *Grafitti Bridge* movie set in Minneapolis, so off I went for a few days of checking in with all things Paisley. I didn't really expect to even see Prince, let alone spend any time with him as he was in total concentration mode, directing and acting in his latest project.

The trip was to give me an opportunity to catch up with the various other projects coming via Paisley Park, as well as some of the music from the soundtrack from the other artists such as George Clinton, Mavis Staples, and Tevin Campbell.

I was in a hallway chatting with someone when, out of the blue (would I EVER learn how he did that?), Prince appeared and asked me to follow him. Okey dokey, here we go again. Perhaps we're off to see the wizard? He looked back a couple of times to make certain I was following him.

We ended up in a small room where there was a playback

machine. Having worked in the movie side of things (at Warner Bros. Pictures), at least I knew what this machine was.

Suddenly, he put his gloved hand in front of the screen and said "Don't Look". Okayyyy.... What am I not looking at, as it's a blank screen? I played along as he fiddled with something in the back. He reminded me, "Don't Look". Honest, I promise I won't.

All of a sudden, he said, "LOOK". A bit of footage showed up on the screen for me to see. As soon as it started, he went back to the "Don't Look" command. After a few seconds, I was told to LOOK again, don't look, look.... I was getting dizzy. Each time he said, "don't look", his gloved hand flew over the screen to block the image from me. It was starting to dawn on me that he was trying to show me some VERY specific pieces of footage without letting me see pieces he wanted to keep private at that point.

I was used to going to dailies, but this footage was right out of the camera and just shot. Years later, I can't remember exactly what footage he was so keen for me to see. I do remember, at the end, him asking me, "So what do you think?" Should I "speak" or "not speak"? I remember that the bits were so confusing and out of order that I wasn't sure what I was seeing. Whatever it was apparently was hilarious, as Prince was slapping his knee and laughing telling me how funny this was.

Okay, time to say "Yep, it's funny". While I wasn't sure what WAS funny, it was the right answer. "I knew you'd get it", he said.

Hmmm.....

A typical video playback machine

To this day I can remember his gloved hand (he had just come in from a ride on his motorcycle), fingers spread wide, flying up over the screen as he said "don't look". The first time he did it, I was more than a little startled! Within seconds, the hand would come back down as he told me to "look".

Thieves in the Temple

I had now absorbed and survived my "look, don't look" encounter.

It was the next day and the movie continued to be filmed. I stayed at Paisley Park until around 8 p.m. (early in the Paisley world). I came back in around 8:30 the next morning and discovered that Prince had never left.

I was on the phone and he appeared at my door. I quickly excused myself from the phone call, as it was clear he had something he wanted to say. Prince said he had something he wanted to play for me. So once again, I followed him to whatever treasure he had waiting. Off to see yet another wizard. Was I up to it?

I entered his studio, and he proceeded to play "Thieves in the Temple". Of special note: this was something he had written, produced, sung, and finished overnight while some of us mortals were sleeping.

When I raved about the quality of the song and the fact that it could reach #1 (be careful about what you promise, as his mind was like a steel trap), he lamented that he had JUST written it and it wasn't in the movie (*Graffiti Bridge*). I felt strongly about the song, and so I told him, "I trust you. You'll find a way to write it into the movie". Of course, he did just that, and it became the strongest piece in the production.

The irony is that the song was about his breakup with Kim Basinger, and as a result it really didn't have any place in the movie. But the song was too good. It needed a forum and the movie was the perfect place.

Once again, he had shown how prolific he was. It was a story I had heard many times, and now I had witnessed it myself.

I Get Delirious... Again

It had been a long day at Paisley Park, and I was headed off to have Chinese food with some of the band.

But first, George Clinton had invited Billy Sparks and me to his hotel room to have a drink with him and some of his friends. George was always loads of fun, so we took him up on it.

A colorful collection of his crew were kicking back and enjoying a nice smoke, drinks, and laughs all around. I was immediately asked if I wanted to share a bit of the smoke, but I decided it probably wasn't a good idea, especially since I had to drive on to the restaurant after stopping here.

We shared some wine and great jokes before we finally needed to take our leave. Being more than just a little naïve, I walked out thinking that I was feeling especially good. It never occurred to me that you can actually get a "contact high", made extremely easy with the amount of weed being smoked in the room. I must say it smelled very nice!

I didn't really realize how high I was until...

You're Under Arrest

I got in the car, giggling and quite happy, ready to strap in and head for the Chinese restaurant and an evening of fun and good food. Billy piled in as well.

Prince had given us a cassette (remember those?) of "Thieves in the Temple", so I had it cranked all the way up in the rental car, singing along with it. Life was good!

Hmmm... Police sirens behind me! I figured they must be after someone else so I kept going. Billy urged me to stop. "But I haven't done anything wrong" (the weed was starting to speak for me, although I didn't realize it at the time).

So, I decided to stop. A local Minneapolis policeman came to the side of the car and said, "Do you have any idea how fast you were going?" I replied very flippantly, "Oh, I don't know, somewhere around the speed limit?"

"No," he replied. "You were going about 60 in a 35 miles-per-hour zone."

I just started giggling again and asked him if he had heard the new song "Thieves in the Temple". I should have definitely tweaked to the fact that I had a contact high. The song had just been written the night before. Meanwhile, Billy was starting to shrink further into the passenger seat and knocking me with his arm.

The policeman looked across at him and then at me and demanded my driver's license. I dutifully handed it over and the cop went back to his car to check it out.

I then got a lecture from Billy. "Don't you know that there are some police in Minnesota who might have a problem with a black man and a white woman travelling together?"

I was stunned at even the thought of the slightest bit of racism (I told you I was naïve). I began to sober up quickly. We waited and waited. It seemed this policeman was determined to find SOMETHING so he could take us in. Thankfully, there was nothing.

He finally returned to the car with a speeding ticket and said, "You better pay this by tomorrow or we will come looking for you."

Phew… That ordeal was over and so was my contact high.

We finally reached the restaurant, and the entire group looked up and wanted to know what took us so long to get there.

It turned into a great story to tell over dinner and funny in retrospect.

Is the Air Warm Enough? YES!

Anyone who has been to Minneapolis in wintertime knows how extraordinarily cold it is.

Unfortunately for me (I hate cold weather), *Graffiti Bridge* was shooting in February and you can't get much colder than that. So, I took my full-length fur coat (I have long since divested myself of any real fur coats, so no hate mail please).

Parts of the Paisley Park complex were not heated, as they were designed for storage, etc., so I avoided those areas. Well, I had done that until...

Prince had set up a small screening area for dailies (usually at the end of a day's shooting, the director and other key people look at all the footage shot on that day to make certain everything was okay) in a corner of the building upstairs. For whatever reason, it was an incredibly cold little area.

He was all set to go look at the day's shooting when he invited me along. I was quite happy to join him, as he was usually pretty private about such things. I just hoped it wouldn't be another "Don't look" moment!

Luckily, I had my coat on as I sat down next to him in a folding chair. Billy Sparks, Morris Day and Jerome Benton were also there. He directed the projector person to start. I let out a BIG shiver as it was freezing! He yelled, "STOP". Oh no, here we go again.

Prince got up and disappeared. The four of us sitting there wondered what had happened. After a few minutes, he reappeared carrying a portable floor heater! He placed it in front me and plugged it in, searching for an extension cord. Not a word was spoken and I was speechless. He yelled, "START".

A few seconds into the scene, I shivered again (honest, I couldn't help it). Prince yelled, "STOP". Off he went again. At this point, Morris and Jerome were giving me a very strange look. "Hey, aren't you cold?" I asked. They just laughed and said I was not used to Minneapolis cold.

Next thing you know, here came Prince again with yet another space heater, cord trailing behind! He very carefully placed the heater on the other side of me so that I would be blasted from both sides. Again, no words were spoken. As soon as he found another outlet, he sat down and yelled, "START".

Seriously, I was starting to warm up but I shivered once again. Oh no. He yelled, "STOP" once again! I quickly told him I was okay, REALLY. Not a word from him, but he disappeared yet again. After almost 10 minutes he trudged up the stairs with yet ANOTHER floor heater. Where was he getting them? Once he hooked this one up, I was surrounded.

Well, you can imagine what happened. I had three heaters coming at me at full strength. I started sweating. Billy, Jerome and Morris started laughing uncontrollably as only they can, pointing at the beads of sweat on my forehead. Morris was at his finest, with his crazy laugh. Prince was literally laughing and rolling on the floor but not at me. He was screaming, "Isn't this hilarious, isn't this great?" He was referring to the hot chili pepper scene in the movie, which was what we were watching.

I was thinking how appropriate, as I now felt like a hot chili pepper. In the middle of his laughter, Prince looked up at me from the floor and asked if I was warmer now.

Yes, Prince, I'm properly cooked. Just turn me over and I'll be done.

She's Got the Look

My Warner Bros. duties covered the USA only, so I wasn't out touring with acts overseas except for rare occasions such as a couple of USO tours we filmed for Black Entertainment Television (BET) specials.

Prince had set off on his NUDE tour, and I got a call from

Minneapolis to ask if I'd like to come along for a bit of the European leg and use vacation time. It took me about two seconds to make up my mind! I flew to Frankfurt, Germany, to hook up with everyone. The moment I reached the hotel I saw a couple of my favorite Paisley Park people and knew I was in for a great couple of weeks.

After the show in Mannheim, we flew to Gothenburg, Sweden. So far, so good. Lots of laughs and amazing music. However, it all changed at Gothenburg customs and immigration. The band, all acting crazy as normal, sailed through immigration. The officers zeroed in on me. After all, here's this "normal-looking" person in business attire. She must be the drug mule for the group! So, I was taken into a side room, where my luggage was literally ripped apart, everything spilled onto the floor, and even my Walkman (yes, youngsters, prior to iPod) was taken apart.

Frustrated that they couldn't find anything after an hour of searching, they finally allowed me to exit. I figured I was on my own in finding my way to the hotel as the band and crew would definitely NOT have waited. I was wrong! There was the band bus, with everyone inside grumbling. I certainly got the third degree. Where WAS I for all that time? I handed them my ruined Walkman and told them all about my experience. I was kidded about that for the rest of the journey.

Yodel O-E-O-E-O

We had moved on from Sweden with no further incidents to Lausanne, Switzerland, where we stayed at a simply gorgeous hotel right on Lake Geneva. Now we're talking! Here we would have a couple of off days while the trucks with all the staging and equipment travelled by road and ferry from Sweden to Switzerland.

We all enjoyed THIS hotel!

The band and tour management received an invitation from the legendary Claude Nobs to spend a day at his home high in the Swiss Alps. Claude was the founder and general manager of the Montreux Jazz Festival (if you want to read about his fascinating background, go to Wikipedia for some interesting facts about him).

There was no question that everyone wanted to go. Claude's

private funicular (yes, he had a private train up the side of the mountain) was too small to accommodate us all, so we sang and swerved around the treacherous corners climbing up, up and away in a minivan. Claude's home wasn't just any house in the mountains. It was a gorgeous chalet filled with an eclectic selection of furniture and items reminiscent of the '50s, '60s and '70s. And there were big screens and sound systems everywhere.

Claude Nob's Swiss Chalet high in the mountains overlooking Lake Geneva

Because he loved inviting musicians to his home, Claude had instruments at the ready just in case someone wanted a casual jam. A grand piano sat in the middle of a room with very high ceilings, mirrors everywhere, and ornate furniture.

A separate building was actually hermetically sealed and housed thousands of recordings – audio, video, LPs and more. You can imagine how the band was awestruck with the entire experience.

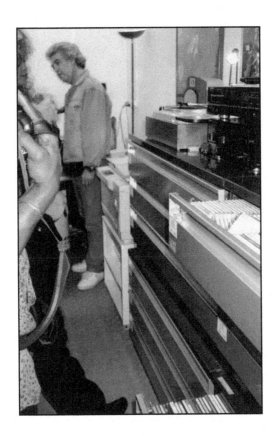

Claude had helpers everywhere running a very fancy barbeque outside while we soaked in the stunning view to Lake Geneva far below.

At one point, Claude made an offer for anyone game enough.... He had a friend who was a European champion in kite flying (of course he did). Did any of us want to jump off the mountain the next day? Some hands went up, including a couple in the band. That's when the tour director put a kibosh on the whole thing. Imagine if one of the band members fell and...

You get the idea. Oh well, it sounded like another fun day!

Just when we thought it was time to pile back into the van, Claude directed us all to take a seat on one of the many benches overlooking the world below. Next thing we knew, the fireworks show started! We were speechless. A private fireworks show over Lake Geneva at the chalet of Claude Nobs. Does it get any better? Probably

Band members Miko Weaver, Rosie Gaines, and Damon Dickson. Looks like they are enjoying their day in the Alps!

Tony M creating a movie (boy, look at the size of that personal video camera!) In the background is tour manager Mark Adelman

Right: Benches overlooking the beautiful Lake Geneva far below. The setting for our personal fireworks show!

Below: Some of us walked up the hill behind the house to capture the breathtaking view with Claude's home in the foreground

Nice Can Be So Nice

I had been thoroughly enjoying being out on this segment of the NUDE tour. But soon it was time to return to reality and my job back in Los Angeles.

At this last stop for me, I decided to stay with the crew instead of the band. (All tours have a less expensive hotel set for the crew who did all the set builds and breakdowns, sound, lights, etc.) I really enjoyed their company and decided it would be great to spend an off day with them in Nice, France. We had a wonderful time in the markets together.

On the last evening, outside his dressing room, Prince and I got into a "deep and meaningful" about the Iraq war that was going on not so very far away. He was always very informed about current events, being a keen observer, watching CNN, and reading newspapers – and he had strong views. I always enjoyed that kind of discussion with him. We were cut short when, all of a sudden, he saw someone approaching from WAY down the long hallway. I couldn't even tell who it was from this distance, but Prince, in a flash, was in his dressing room with the door shut. It turned out to be a major recording artist with whom Prince, for whatever reasons, did not want to interact.

I had seen him from time to time when he wanted to avoid someone. He was excellent at the disappearing act. He had it perfected!

At that moment, I could not have realized that the next time I was in Nice, France, in April of 2016 on holiday, I would be rocked with the news of Prince's death.

Party Up

The Warner Bros. Records building had been designed in a way that allowed for concerts (as well as employee gatherings) to be held on its main patio. Through the years, many Warner Bros. artists would perform on the patio JUST for the WBR employees! I saw many an incredible "private" show on that patio with Seal, Ice T, Al Jarreau, Doobie Bros, Rod Stewart, k.d. Lang, Eric Clapton, and Chaka Khan to name a few.

One particular day at Warner Bros. Records was already a VERY special one for me, as my promotion to Vice President was being announced. I had worked long and hard over many years, and I was extremely excited.

But leave it to Prince to make it even more special. As people began arriving at their desks on this particular Monday morning in

June, everyone discovered an unusual piece of paper taped to their desk.

To the delight of all, Prince was planning a surprise concert on the patio at noon. The anticipation was palpable. And here I thought this day was "just" going to be my promotion!

As it happened, my office at the time was adjacent to the patio, so it became "Prince Central". As the band members and Paisley support staff started arriving, they were piling into my office (small under the best of circumstances, but now you couldn't move). The band decided to use my office as their dressing room. Okay, once again I had lost control.

My office just off the patio (which I loved)

I could see I would get nothing done that morning. But then I don't think ANYONE in the building was working. Everyone was running around awaiting not only the concert but maybe a glimpse of the man himself when he arrived.

His crew had arrived very early in the morning, and the full sound and lighting setup was being installed. Just because it was a patio and a private concert didn't mean any corners would be cut. After all, this was Prince!

I continued to watch everything unfold from my "front row seat" (my office). I jokingly told the band how nice it was for Prince and them to come perform for my promotion.

Noon finally arrived. The patio had long since filled up with all the people in the building, as they jostled to get as close to the stage as possible.

Prince came out in a bright orange outfit, perfect for the sunny day, and the band rocked the house. At one point, I looked across the street where there was a building several stories high. For the first time ever, people were hanging out the windows, soaking in the music. In all the patio performances I had attended I had never seen that before!

Photographer unknown

The show ended and Prince quickly disappeared. The band members stayed around to chat with people. The mood was incredible.

Indeed, we partied like it was 1999 and absolutely no work was done that day.

Oh, and the press release about my promotion was issued.

You Want Me To Do WHAT?

Many Prince fans know that he would always come up with something "special" around his birthday each year. It might be anything from a special concert to a private party to…

His thirty-third birthday was coming up, and his brainstorm for that year was a 12-inch EP (Extended Play) vinyl record of "Gett Off", which he would personally deliver to clubs around Los Angeles and then farther afield. This version would include a "Damn near 10 minute" mix (I'm not kidding – that's what it was called) of the funky song, which would not be available ANYWHERE else. The song was on the *Diamonds And Pearls* album but not any sort of remix.

Sounded harmless enough, right? It would have been, except he wanted to drag me right into the middle by having me organize the pressing and manufacture of 1500 copies. So, what was the problem, you ask. He wanted it completely "under the radar", so Warner Bros. was not to know about it or be involved in any way. Didn't he know who I worked for? I kept saying no. That was a word he simply didn't understand OR accept.

Somehow (to this day I'm not sure how), he managed to get me to say "yes". I found a small pressing plant in Santa Monica, California, that agreed to do it and keep it under wraps.

What was I thinking?

In the Midnight Hour

I arranged to have 1500 copies delivered to my home and put them in the garage to "await further instructions". Within a day I received a call from Duane Nelson, Prince's half-brother, who was working as his bodyguard at the time. They (whoever "they" were) would come by my home around midnight for the product.

Okey-dokey. All I can say is it was a good thing that the neighbors were asleep, as a stretch black limo pulled up in front of the house around midnight and Duane jumped out of the car. He and I carried the boxes and loaded them into the trunk. If a neighbor had witnessed this they probably would have called the police! At that point, I had no idea Prince was also in the car, as the dark windows were closed.

We were down to the last boxes when Duane said, "Keep a box for yourself. They will be worth a lot of money one day". At that point, the window rolled down, and Prince looked out and just smiled. They pulled off, heading for the clubs so that Prince could deliver his birthday 12-inch to all the hot spots.

Ironically, as weird as I felt about this little escapade, this 12-inch blew up in the clubs. As a result, "Gett Off" (without the "Damn near 10 minute" version) was officially released as a 7-inch and a 12-inch, becoming a #1 US Billboard Hot Dance Club hit, Top 10 on the

R&B Chart and Top 25 on the Hot 100 chart! PHEW – saved by the hit!

This version went on to become quite a collector's item. Oh, and I still have some of those that were given to me.

Sealed with Spit

Yes, Prince had a unique sense of humour. He loved to play pranks and would crack himself up with some of his shenanigans. He could be his own best audience.

I had been at home after being quite ill. While I was on the mend, I was feeling sorry for myself and not answering the phone. I hadn't been to work for a while as I recovered.

The front doorbell rang, and I remember feeling put out that I had to get up and answer it.

Lo and behold, it was a large box of cut flowers, all very exotic, but without a card to tell me who sent them. Hmm... Because they had not come arranged in a vase, I had to spend time doing that myself. I must say it cheered me up a bit.

The next day more exotic flowers arrived in the same manner. Once again, I was forced to find a vase and arrange them.

This went on for at least another day or two before the light went on in my brain. They had to be coming from the jokester in Minneapolis.

I rang Paisley Park and asked if they could stop with the flowers because I had run out of vases and the place looked like a funeral home! There was much laughter on the other end of the phone as it was explained that the flowers would have kept coming until I got up and out of my deep funk.

Mission accomplished! Oh, and there was finally a card....

Not happy with just sending flowers, he next sent a handwritten note. It touched me deeply that Prince would take the time to send such a card.

But in his unique way, he had to do something that would absolutely crack me up. A completely handwritten card, with his famous doodles arrived ... Note the back of the envelope: "sealed with spit".

I still laugh over that one to this day! Turn to the next page and I think you'll have a chuckle as well!

MARYloU

SEALED With SPIT

"Love You"

It's hard to know
what to say
when an illness is so serious,
but hope you know
you're being thought about
with special love.

Prince -90-91

New Position

Prince and I were having a casual talk one day at Paisley Park. Chats with him were typically very brief, as he was always heading back into the studio and didn't like to "waste time" chatting. You could be in the middle of a sentence, turn, and he was gone. Some music was swirling in his head, no doubt.

This time, as he turned to leave, he said, "You should come work for me". Of course, I was flattered; however, I knew that would be one of the greatest mistakes I could ever make. First, I had a great job working for a really terrific organization, with many opportunities. Second, as anyone who has spent time around entertainers, actors, and the like knows, it can be a 24/7 job at the whim of that person.

Finally, Prince wasn't just any entertainer. I had often thought how amazing the people who worked for him were in that he slept so little and was so demanding. You would be at his beck and call and could be out the door in a flash. He was a perfectionist in every way, not only in everything he did but also in what he expected from those around him.

So, how to turn him down without insulting him (if he was even serious about the offer anyway), and respond quickly as he had no patience if you wanted to take time answering. I thanked him but reminded him that I was actually more valuable to him working at the record label. He had talented people working for him, and I was of more use on the "other side". The other key issue was that as long as I wasn't on his payroll, I could say whatever I needed to say without concern over any sort of repercussion.

His look as I answered concerned me. But then he broke into his crooked grin and turned as he walked away. His hand went up and he said, "Yeah, you're right. I always knew you were smart."

Quick Draw

MTV had their World Premiere party in Sheridan, Wyoming, so it was my turn to think of something (bigger and better) for my friends at Black Entertainment Television (BET).

What could be better than to have a contest where not one but TEN lucky winners would fly to London to see the DIAMONDS AND PEARLS concert AND meet the band in a party backstage after the show! The next challenge was to make it work, moneywise.

After some fast talk to American Airlines and a few other possible co-sponsors, we were ON!

Ten (and a guest) VERY excited winners were off to London.

I flew to London a couple of days ahead of the winners in order to make their stay the best it could be. I ran around and got maps, tourist brochures and anything else I could think of.

Then it was off to a soundcheck to meet up with with the band. A soundcheck, for those who don't know, is something that happens on the afternoon of the show. It gives the band and all the technicians the chance to test the sound and lighting, and then make any and all adjustments needed to ensure the show goes as smoothly as possible.

In Prince's case, soundchecks were NOT open to anyone outside the key personnel. I was extremely fortunate that I was welcome to come in and watch. For Prince, the soundcheck was often a place to test new music (which might never see the light of day) or have a jam. It all depended on his mood. Through the years I heard some pretty amazing jams in that special environment. It was always a real treat to see when it was all coming together, as he would sit at the piano, furiously playing something amazing, his eyes closed and in another world.

How often I wondered what that world was like!

Anyway, back to the soundcheck. I was sitting in the first row just enjoying the music when Prince came down from the stage straight towards me. Was he going to kick me out of soundcheck? Instead, he handed me his famous microphone gun that he was using at the time. I wasn't sure what I was supposed to do with it – "shoot" him or? I looked it over and he finally said, "So, what do you think?" Again, that could mean a myriad of things, as you just never knew with him. I handed it back and just said, "Very nice". He laughed, said "Yup", spun on his feet, and disappeared back up to the stage where he continued right from where he had left off.

The winners had been having a ball in London when it was time to go to the show and then the after-party. The winners were deliriously happy as they met and took pictures with the band members. It was a very successful few days for all.

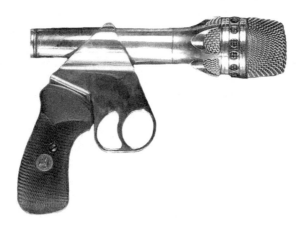

The famous "Gun Microphone"

Clowning around backstage with the band

Let's Work!

Prince was now a Vice President of Warner Bros. Records, a part of his new contract. There were a few execs within the halls of the record company who scoffed at this, but Prince was adamant about the title being part of his new deal.

It was 1993, and he convened a meeting with several executives at Warner Bros. Records in a large conference room. He wanted an update on what was being done to promote his projects, including an "ABC in Concert" gig that was coming up on ABC Television. *

Around the very large conference table, one after another, various execs filled him in on what their respective areas of the company were doing for him. Through no specific plan, I was sitting directly across from Prince, albeit at quite a distance (there must have been at least 25 seated at that big round table).

I continued to look across at Prince as he listened, without comment, to the folks proudly relating their contributions to promotion, advertising, marketing, international exposure, and all else "Prince". He looked across to me, as each one spoke, with a look of consternation. He was well known (at least within his "circle") for that as his "get to something important as this is not doing it for me" look.

There were those who spoke up and indicated they could do

"more" if he would be more available and approachable (a never-ending challenge with him). Those comments got the same look and didn't go anywhere. Understand that through all of this, he had not spoken ONE word! That can be off-putting at best. He had a unique style of intimidation that he had truly mastered.

I could see that everything was falling flat, so I spoke up. While I could never say that I knew him well enough to always get things right around him (no one was that lucky), I would speak up when I felt I had something that MIGHT hit a good note with him (while also making sense from the record company's point of view).

In this case, I simply said, "If you'd just give me access to some footage ("ABC in Concert" footage), I can get a spot cut overnight and aired on BET at no cost" (BET = Black Entertainment Television). An exec sitting next to me kicked me under the table as if to say, "Are you crazy asking for something he'll never give you?"

Prince immediately broke into a small smile and said, "Meet me at the studio at 7:30 tonight and you can have anything you want". VICTORY! The room fell silent. At that point, he simply got up and walked out of the room with nothing more to say.

No one said anything to me, but a couple of people looked at me sideways.

I headed back to my office with the challenge of delivering

what I promised. Fortunately, I had a great relationship with BET, and especially as it was Prince-related I knew I could get the help I needed. It didn't hurt that a very talented BET producer and personal friend had just moved to Los Angeles and was temporarily staying at my home until she could find her own place.

Of course, she was totally down to do the spot and cleared her evening. I suggested we go out and have a nice dinner and then head over to the studio. She loved the idea and was thrilled that she would have the opportunity to meet Prince.

We got to chatting (as we always did) and lost track of the time. When she looked at her watch she panicked, as we couldn't make the 7:30 time. I told her not to worry, as he wouldn't be ready for me anyway. We set off and arrived at the recording studio at 8 pm. I announced our arrival with the receptionist. She told me that Prince had come out looking for me and told her to send me back the moment I got there. Whoops, I should have known!

We arrived in his studio, and he immediately stopped doing what he was doing and was so gracious in meeting the producer. He even thanked her for taking the time to do it, saying with a chuckle, "I'm sure Marylou didn't give you a choice".

We sat down to look at the footage and he announced, "Why don't you take it all and use what you want". I explained that we'd be several hours and how did he want me to get the spot to him for approval. He waved his hand and said, "Don't worry about it. I trust you". EEK. This had better be good!

We headed off to the BET studio in Burbank to work on the spot, finishing up around 6 a.m. I definitely felt sleep-deprived! The spot immediately went into heavy rotation on the network.

I never heard back from Prince about the spot, but that was fine. It fell into the "no news is good news" basket.

* It should be noted that Warner Bros. did not organize the "ABC in Concert" gig. We didn't book it, as it was organized directly by Prince's people at Paisley Park.

Thieves in MY Temple

Through the years of working with Prince and the Paisley people, I was fortunate to have been given tour jackets from several tours, such as PURPLE RAIN and many others. They all had my name embroidered on the front.

In addition, the wardrobe department made a suit for me as well as a shirt that matched one Prince wore in *Under the Cherry Moon.*

One day I returned from work and on first glance would never have guessed someone had been in my home. I went to the closet where these items were kept and the section was EMPTY! Someone had broken in, taken ONLY these items, and left with no clues whatsoever.

I was devastated and tried, over a long period of time, to find them as the jackets all had my name on them.

To this day, the jackets have never surfaced. I am really happy that my gold and platinum records were not taken, as I still have and treasure them.

The suit made for me by
the wardrobe department

I Wish You Heaven

Prince's generosities have really only started to become known since his death. He performed many acts of kindness and did NOT want them to be known. I admired that in him, as so many famous people make certain everyone knows what they do, almost turning it into a "look how great I am" sort of scenario.

Behind the scenes, he helped people struggling financially, artistically, and every other way. Those closest to him were really the only ones who had a sense of this side of him, and you just KNEW not to speak of it.

I'm sure there were constant requests fielded by Paisley Park in Minneapolis for donations, charity performances, and the like. I received some myself, referring only a few up to Minneapolis.

There was one time when the Make-A-Wish Foundation contacted me. Their initial contact was a letter in which they told me about a young lady (about 13 years old) who was extremely ill in the hospital with not a lot of time left. She never spoke, had no expression with her eyes closed, but lay there listening to Prince music all the time. Her mother made a request on her behalf to have Prince visit her.

While I knew that was an impossible ask, I had an idea. I rang the Foundation representative and explained that a visit would not be possible, but IF I could secure an autographed picture (Prince rarely autographed anything) AND the Foundation could promise that this would not be made public, would that suffice? They indicated that would be amazing, and of course they would honour his wish to keep anything he did a secret.

And, so, I contacted Minneapolis and asked if Prince would sign a picture and I would get it to the people at Make-a-Wish.

A few days later a "personal and confidential" envelope arrived at my office. I opened it up and there was a thick envelope inside that had not been sealed. What is this, I wondered? I opened it up and in Prince's handwriting there was a personal letter several pages long to this young girl! He explained that as much as he would like to visit, he was on tour and couldn't make it. However, he was thinking of her and was so happy that she loved to listen to his music. I was absolutely stunned at this wonderful and personal letter!

I put it back in its envelope, sealed it, and made arrangements to hand it over personally to the Foundation representative.

A few days later I received a phone call from Make-a-Wish. The woman could barely talk, as she was so emotional. They had taken the letter to the hospital for the girl's mom to read to her. As mom was reading, the girl opened her eyes for the first time in weeks and actually smiled. About an hour later, she passed away, still with a smile on her face.

What may have seemed a small gesture was stunning in its

unselfishness. All I asked for was a signed photograph, which would have taken a few seconds. Instead, Prince spent a good deal of time composing and writing a letter by hand to a girl who loved his music and was soon to leave this earth. And, typical to Prince, there were some of his famous doodles on the pages. With this kindness from Prince, she left with a smile on her face.

Got Any Pheromone?

Prince fans will of course be familiar with the "Pheromone" cut on the *Come* album released in 1994.

The song actually started its life as an instrumental in 1993 as the theme for Black Entertainment Television's (BET) *Video LP* show, a half-hour, live viewer call-in program on the network.

But HOW did it become the theme song?

BET had long been a strong supporter of Prince. In fact, BET had, over the years, helped break many Warner Bros. artists (as well as artists on other labels). As a result, BET was a very important part of any marketing campaign. Time after time, the great people there were supportive of our new black acts and open to really pushing new artists.

Where MTV wouldn't touch black artists in general, BET was there, giving strong rotation, doing interviews, airing specials, and generally being a terrific help.

They were the first and only outlet (other than some local music video outlets) to play Prince from his very first video, "I Wanna Be Your Lover" in 1979.

I had many friends within BET, often being invited to home parties and generally being part of the "posse". Many are still friends today.

We at Warner Bros. Black Music felt so strongly about their importance that we hosted the BET 10th Anniversary television special, which was held on the Warner Bros. patio. It was an amazing tribute attended by many members of the Warner Bros. artist roster including Morris Day (The Time), Michael McDonald (Doobie Bros.), Isley Bros., Mavis Staples, El Debarge and many more. Not only were there special video montages of our artists, but several performed live in this two-hour special. We initiated the BET Walk of Fame. For this, I asked Prince to donate something. And boy did he come through – handwritten lyrics to one of his hits, framed and ready to hang!

WARNER SALUTES BET WITH A BLACK TIE AFFAIR

In celebration of BET's 10th Anniversary, Warner Bros. Records hosted a Black Tie party. The evening was kicked off with perform by Ronald Isley, David Peaston and Joe Sample. Donnie Simpson was later greeted by various Warner Bros. artists durii taping of his "Video Soul" program.

PAGE 14 / MARCH 16, 1990

The above excerpt from *Black Radio Exclusive* (BRE) is included with the permission of Sydney Miller, Publisher. My thanks to him and his magazine for all their support through the years to Warner Bros. Black Music.

Hanging with the one and only Morris Day of the Time. What great memories working with these guys!

But, back to the new theme song for BET. One of the producers of *Video LP* indicated that the show was looking for a new theme to be played at the head of the show.

My mind quickly switched to "hmmm... If I could get something from Prince, it would be a major 'thank you' from him for the years of support". Obviously, I didn't say anything, as I really had no idea whether I could pull it off.

So, I went off on a mission of a different kind. My motto had always been "anything (sensible) is worth an ask. If you don't ask, you don't know what you might have accomplished". With this motto in the back of my head, I went to Prince and laid out my idea. I knew at this point he was not interested in doing an interview. However, if he were willing to donate a song (or even a few bars), the network would be VERY grateful and it would be a wonderful way for him to say "thank you" for all the years of support.

To my delight, there was no hesitation. Within days I had an instrumental song, which at that point had no title. I flew to Washington DC to deliver it in person. Everyone at the network was absolutely over the moon. After all, he had not done anything like this for anyone else.

While I don't now remember how many years they used it as the theme, it certainly was appreciated.

A few months later, with lyrics, it was released as the song "Pheromone".

You Too Can Be Interactive

I suspect a lot of Prince fans are not aware of Prince's foray into the Interactive CD-ROM world.

As in everything else, Prince was always ahead of his time, pushing the envelope. We were in the infancy of true interactive games, so this was definitely not like anything else out there – other than "Myst", an interactive game that was very popular.

The people at Paisley Park knew I was very well versed in all things gaming and computers, as I had actually introduced computers to the WB Black Music Department back in the late '70s with the Apple IIe! I was also keenly aware of what was happening in the market gaming-wise.

So, from the perspective viewpoint of Minneapolis, I was the perfect person to pull into this project.

The first challenge was, of course, to find the right gaming company to build and develop what Prince envisioned. That required a few trips to various cities to talk to gaming people. It also had to be a company that was up on the new technology of CD-ROMs.

We finally settled on a young company, Graphix Zone, to do the work. The people there were very excited to be involved, as they were Prince fans. They figured that OF COURSE they would get to meet Prince. In fact, I think they envisioned that Prince would waltz through the doors of their place to sit down with them directly.

Need I say more? The entire project was done via the Paisley

Park representative and me, with all the input and elements provided. They never even spoke to Prince. But in his normal manner, he was monitoring the project and had final say on everything that went into his "virtual world". Once again, he had a clear vision of the final product.

While the game itself received mixed reviews, the project contained six complete songs (three unreleased), four full-length videos, fifty-two song clips, thirty-one video clips, nine morphs, and seventy-six animations along with the required challenges (eleven in all). Once you solved all the mysteries in Prince's world, you got access to a special treat in the Dome Room. Once again, Prince was on the cutting edge.

At the moment, you can see the complete game at:

 https://www.youtube.com/watch?v=rDFXlYfEHuI

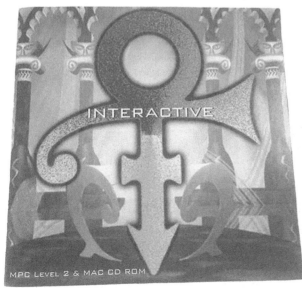

Release It... Please!

It was common knowledge that Prince was prolific in his writing and recording of music. The music was never-ending, and other artists benefitted from his wealth of material as well.

He invited me into the studio one evening to listen to a couple of new songs he had written, recorded, mixed, and finished in a 24-hour period. I don't know of anyone else that prolific.

I honestly don't even remember the exact songs he played for me, but he danced, twirled, and watched me for my reaction.

In the middle of the second song, he stopped the playback and walked up to me so we were truly face-to-face (in his heels he was the same height as I am in flats).

I will NEVER forget the expression on his face as he told me to "go back to Warner Bros. and tell them they need to release my music faster". Oh boy, back in the middle of something I don't want to be in the middle of. I did my best to explain to him that the people who buy his records cannot absorb them as quickly as he makes them.

He stood there, the most plaintive expression in his eyes – an expression I remember to this day. "What am I supposed to do?" Prince lamented. "The music just flows through me. I can't control it". I had heard of this phenomenon but had never encountered it directly before. Obviously, when you don't have this "talent" (not sure if it's a wonderful thing or a curse), it is pretty impossible to understand it. Imagine waking in the middle of the night with music and/or imagery going through your mind. You're unable to sleep until you paint it, write it, create it.

My creative side could empathize with his feelings. Imagine if you are a painter or a writer and you just can't stop the creative flow. Imagine that you are at odds with those who make certain your creation(s) are seen and/or heard. You NEED your creation out there and not sitting in a vault or back room so it can be shared with the world. But the people can't absorb your art as fast as you create it. What a difficult position to be in!

This was a big part of what created the rift between Prince and Warner Bros., along with the ownership of the masters, which of course was a MAJOR point of contention. Again, there is an argument for either side. As the creator of the music (or artwork, or any other creative "thing"), you want ownership. After all, YOU created it.

However, you have signed an agreement with a company that is equipped with the wherewithal to get it out there, heard (or seen), and to sell it. Of course, they have also fronted the money to record, tour, and much more. They need to have a return on their investment. And, we won't even go into all the artists who were signed, given money, and never made it so the company took a loss.

You could argue that one artist should not have to "pay" for another's failure and that's true. But imagine the huge risk a company such as Warner Bros. takes every time they sign an artist, send them into the studio, put the promotion and marketing machine behind them, make a video, provide distribution, and the list goes on and on. Prince was no exception in his early albums, as they certainly were not commercial successes when initially released. But Warner Bros. NEVER swayed from their total and complete belief in him. The WB checkbook remained open.

Of course, we all understand that the entire model has changed since the internet has opened up major avenues of exposure for any artist who wants to record. And, the recording can now be done on computers in an artist's garage. But except for the rare few, it's pretty impossible to get through the massive amounts of "music" that is out there. A record company does that for the artist and at tremendous cost.

It's a real conundrum that still exists today. While I was happy that there was no follow-up conversation to his plea to me, through the ensuing years he did a great deal for artists' rights.

The Most Beautiful Girl

If someone were to ask, "if you only had one pick, what would you choose as the highlight of your career?"

For me it was, without a doubt, being acknowledged by Prince (at the time he was only known as "the symbol") as having been an influence on his career! WOW.

To be acknowledged by any artist is extremely flattering, but to be singled out by an artist of Prince's stature was something I just can't put into words. For me, a career at a label with the excellence of Warner Bros. was enough in itself. For most, working in the music industry lets you be close to the music you love and, with a bit of luck, make a difference in the careers of the artists you work with. Anything beyond that is truly a bonus.

I received a phone call from Minneapolis telling me of this award and that there would be a luncheon a few weeks down the track. Not only would my trip be paid for, but I could take someone as my guest.

I had a good friend who was a young musician and a massive Prince fan living in Washington DC, so I decided that he would be the one to accompany me for the weekend. Paisley Park was gracious in agreeing to pay for two hotel rooms.

The weekend arrived, so off I went. Not only was I very excited about the luncheon itself, but I would once again have a chance to catch up with many of my wonderful Paisley friends.

The weekend was non-stop fun, and my musician friend enjoyed every minute. I took him to the Paisley Park facility so he could have a private tour and see the iconic Studio A where Prince recorded.

We joined several friends for dinner at a place that I just couldn't seem to get to. All I could do was find a one-way street going the wrong way with speed bumps. So, after a few turns around the area and not finding a street where I could access the restaurant, I decided we would speed down the one-way street the wrong way. We flew over the speed bumps. My friend said, "What are you doing?" I simply replied, "Well, they are SPEED bumps!" Perhaps any time I went to Minneapolis, the air was filled with that George Clinton contact high.

The luncheon was intimate and lovely. While Prince was on tour, some of the people from Paisley came, as well as Prince's mother. My dear and close friend Billy Sparks, who had worked for and with Prince for years, introduced me. Billy even brought his wife, Valerie, whom I had spoken to MANY times on the phone but had never had the joy of meeting.

An incredibly special weekend, and an incredibly special

With Billy Sparks
Remember him in PURPLE RAIN?
And, below, the plaque which I display to this day

It's Gonna Be a Beautiful Night

I had left the industry and made my way to Australia in 2001, knowing it was time to shift gears. I departed Warner Bros. Records at the time of the merger between Time/Warner and AOL. It was going to be a very different company, adapting to a very different industry as streaming and the internet had taken over.

People would often ask me, "Do you miss it?" The short answer has always been, "I miss what it was, not what it is today".

But even though I had purposely left the industry I loved so much, it didn't change how I felt about the music and artists.

When I heard Prince was coming to Australia, I didn't hesitate when offered tickets to go to his upcoming show in Brisbane. While I hadn't talked with Prince in some time, I really appreciated the fact that there were four tickets for me. I couldn't wait to soak in the music and atmosphere as a "fan" and not have to run around backstage.

With a couple of friends in tow, I could immediately see and feel the electricity in the air. Nothing had changed from years ago, as the filled arena waited on the edge of their collective seats for the first note.

And typical of every show Prince ever performed, the moment he walked onstage the place shook with screaming and anticipation.

"Dearly Beloved..." The crowd ROARED and jumped to their

feet, never sitting down again.

I had as much fun watching the fans watch him as I did being immersed in the music. And did he play the music we all love! It was a set list sent from heaven, as he stretched across the years. Of course, some personal favourites were missing. The show would have taken days to cover the whole catalogue.

He danced, he spun, and he talked a bit to the audience in a frame of mind that spoke of being happy and relaxed. When he sat down at the piano, he whispered, "so many memories, so little time."

After it was all over, everyone was on a Purple High as they headed back to their cars and reality. My friends, not really understanding the music business, said, "Aren't you disappointed that he didn't reach out to you and say hello?"

I chuckled and replied, "But he did.... He played a couple of bars of "The Most Beautiful Girl in the World" interlaced with several other songs as he sat at the piano. That was my 'hello'!"

I did receive a phone call the next morning where there was this very familiar deep voice on the other end. "Did you like it?", he asked. "Of course!", I replied. He then said, "I said Hello during the show." I replied that I knew he had. With a slight chuckle he hung up the phone.

Setlist – Brisbane Entertainment Centre

1. Let's Go Crazy
2. I Would Die 4 U
3. When Doves Cry
4. Baby I'm a Star
5. Shhh
6. D.M.S.R.
7. A Love Bizarre
8. The Glamorous Life
9. I Feel for You
10. Controversy
11. The Beautiful Ones
12. Nothing Compares 2 U
13. Insatiable
14. Sign "O" the Times
15. The Question of U
16. The Ride
17. Let's Work
18. U Got the Look
19. Life "O" the Party
20. Soul Man
21. Kiss
22. Take Me With U
23. The Everlasting Now

Piano set

24. Anna Stesia
25. Diamonds and Pearls
26. Sometimes It Snows in April
27. Little Red Corvette
28. Raspberry Beret
29. How Come U Don't Call Me Anymore

30. The Most Beautiful Girl in the World

31. A Case of You

32. All the Critics Love U in New York

Encore

33. Alphabet Street

34. The Jam

35. Thank You (Falettinme Be Mice Elf Agin)

36. Days of Wild

Encore 2

37. Purple Rain

Take a Picture Sweetie

I often think back on all the times I could have taken photographs of the many artists I was privileged to work with, but I quickly remind myself of a few facts.

First and foremost (and this will be hard to understand for anyone under a certain age), there were NO cameras built into phones until 2000! In fact, mobile phones themselves are not that old, having been invented in 1973 and costing around $4000 in 1983.

But I digress. Regardless of camera phone technology, I had strong feelings that it would have been "taking advantage" of close proximity, which really wasn't fair.

Those feelings, as well as how strongly Prince felt about pictures being taken of him without permission, are why I simply don't have candid photos. I treasure the photo taken of the two of us in 1979. I have kept most of my laminates, invites, notes from Prince, etc. I have my gold and platinum records, which to this day hang on a wall in my home.

Those are my keepsakes for memories that will be with me forever.

Clockwise from top left:
Beret given me during the Nude Tour in Europe; Promotional Batcan;
Diamonds and Pearls cufflinks; scarf he gave to me during Lovesexy tour

Personally signed poster

Limited Edition Pin

One of the original tambourines and
an original Tamboracca

Left: label from t-shirt from European tour.

Below: Special sweatshirt given out by Production Company

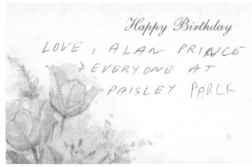

WORLD PREMIERE SCREENING

Graffiti Bridge

Thursday November 1, 1990
8:00 p.m.

Cineplex Odeon
ZIEGFELD
141 West 54th Street
(Between 6th and 7th Avenues)

ADMIT ONE
NON-TRANSFERABLE

Season's Greetings!

Paisley Park

"Love God"

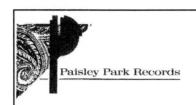

Paisley Park Records

MAVIS STAPLES IS A NATIONAL TREASURE WE ALL SHOULD SHARE.

IN CO-PRODUCING "TIME WAITS FOR NO ONE", I ONLY HOPE TO BRING

TO HER THE ATTENTION AND LOVE THAT SHE SO RICHLY DESERVES.

THANK YOU FOR YOUR SUPPORT.

Love you.
Prince 89

7801 Audubon Road, Chanhassen, MN 55317 • (612) 474-6204 • FAX (612) 474-6328

Prince was a HUGE fan of Mavis Staples and gave this letter to me to get copies of it out with all the Mavis singles being delivered to R&B radio stations around the country. It's well documented that he supported many artists, both known and unknown.

Thanksgiving with the Band on the LOVESEXY Tour
New Orleans – November 24, 1988

My Tour Book Becomes an Amazing Keepsake

Any artist tour is, by its very nature, "insular" from the world, as everyone becomes a family for a period of weeks or months, travelling, eating, and working together day after day.

At the end of a tour, the tour book sometimes becomes like a "high school yearbook" of sorts and is passed around for everyone to sign.

Among my most treasured memories are the many weeks I was on tour with Prince and the band on the LOVESEXY Tour. Because I was there on closing night, I had the opportunity to have my tour book signed as well. Wonderful memories forever!

The cover signed by Prince...

From Miko

Sheila loves to sign things in reverse!

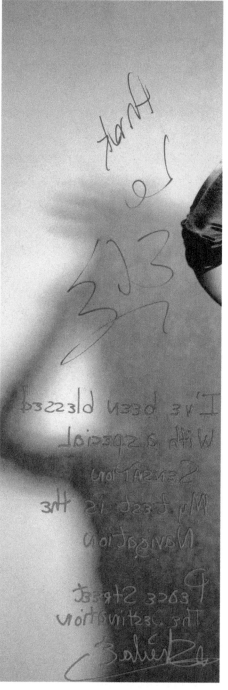

To Mary lou
Thanks for sharing
your expertise and
friendship
Love
Levi Seacer

"88"

Levi Seacer finds a spot on the cover as well…..

The Doctor is in…..

The Great Horn Section of
Eric Leeds and Matt Blisten

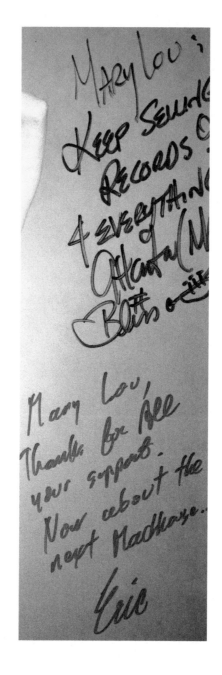

From Cat

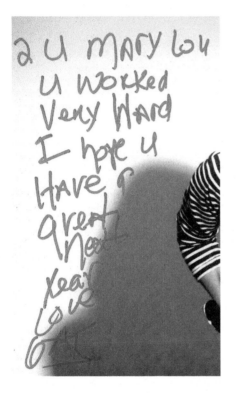

The lovely Miss Bonnie Boyer

On one of my trips to Minneapolis I pulled together the original TIME
for a television documentary special on BET.
What an incredible day with these guys!
Donnie Simpson was the host.

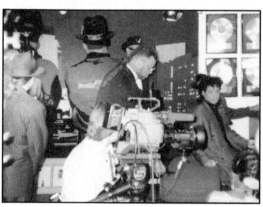

Yes, Sometimes It DOES Snow in April

I was in Nice, France at the beginning of a cruise holiday. Before boarding the ship, we walked through the same area of town I had visited with the Prince crew so many years earlier. I even commented that it was the first time since the NUDE Tour that I had visited Nice.

Once boarded, I began the job of unpacking and readying for dinner. I switched CNN on and was hit between the eyes with the unthinkable news that Prince had died. It was simply incomprehensible to me. I passed on having dinner that first evening as I tried to absorb what I was watching.

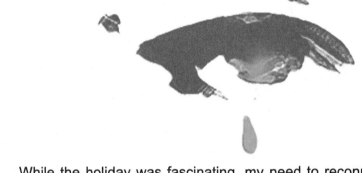

While the holiday was fascinating, my need to reconnect with my Prince friends was uppermost in my mind. Everyone around him felt the same, and we all "talked" incessantly on our Facebook pages as well as private emails flying backwards and forwards. Stories were shared and disbelief turned into sadness. The reconnection did help us all, I believe. In fact, a reunion of those who had worked with him was put together soon after his death. While I was unable to make it, it was clear that everyone who did go had a very healing and special weekend.

I believe we were all overwhelmed by the impact, worldwide, of his death and his legacy. We all knew we had worked for and around a genius but were stunned at the outpouring from every corner of the world.

Over the next few days of my holiday, we visited very small ports where I saw local newspaper after local newspaper with its entire front page dedicated to Prince.

His hauntingly beautiful ballad, "Sometimes it Snows in April", written and performed in 1986, had come to pass.

Front page, even in small villages in France

Moments... Remembering Friends

When I began writing this book it was for the purpose of documenting some of my funny, wonderful, crazy, and life-remembering moments with Prince and his people at Paisley Park. Now I realize the process has created so much more for me than I ever could have understood when I started.

As we go through this thing called "Life", we have little time to stop and think about the people we meet, the situations we encounter, or the lasting effect either or both of those can have on us.

I, like so many, was so busy just trying to do my job that I never took the time out to really appreciate those I met and those who became either friends in a moment of time or friends for life. For some unexplained reason, the people I met because of Prince mostly fall into the latter category and have given me much to be thankful for.

Prince's death, untimely and horrible as it was, threw me abruptly back into the world of Paisley and re-connecting with many I had lost touch with. When that happened, the memories of my relationships with each of them started flooding back into my being. Having that huge vault of memories has been amazing and wonderful – and comforting.

I never kept a journal during my working days, which I now regret. As a result, I have to rely on my memory, so I'm sure I'm forgetting a lot. But there is much I *do* remember, and every memory brings a smile to my face.

While many may not know the names I cite, here is a list of just some of the special moments I remember with the Paisley crew (in no particular order):

Alan and Gwen Leeds – your undying friendship, being invited to your home, more encounters than any of us can remember!

Alan Leeds – Seeing you cross the hotel lobby in 2016 when you visited Australia with D'Angelo. That huge hug and the afternoon in the lobby bar, talking like we had seen one another only the day before... The bonus was the phone conversation with Gwen.

Eric Leeds – travelling to Melbourne last year to renew an old and wonderful friendship. Having dinner with you and Paul Peterson (despite working closely with Paisley Park, I never had the pleasure of meeting Paul when he was with the group "The Family") was one of the best evenings I've spent. So many laughs. And the bonus of seeing your FDeluxe show that evening in front of a very appreciative crowd.

Billy Sparks – what can I say? Like a brother to me, you have always had my back. Many hilarious times together, thousands (yes, thousands) of phone calls. Billy... remember commenting on that couple on the "cheap date"? A running gag for years.

Billy Sparks and Quentin Perry – those conference calls at 2 or 3 in the morning while Prince was on tour (any tour) discussing, fixing issues. We tried to never leave a stone unturned. Then people would wonder why I was so tired when I got to work early the next morning!

Earl Jones (RIP) – the running gag of you behind the stately columns in whatever upscale hotel we were in, regardless of country. It must have had the hotel people curious as you waited for me to come through the doors and you'd jump out at me!

Helen Hiatt – our trek through Frankfurt (I think) looking for a shirt for the boss. Did we ever find it?

Shannon Swedberg (RIP) – your unique friendship. I have pictures of you in my den with my dogs when you gave me that beautiful little china rabbit to mark our friendship. Then there was that wonderful weekend at your place when we went riding. You were always so kind.

Therese Stoulil – what can I say… You always called me "Mar" and it seemed to suit our friendship perfectly. If my office told me you were on the phone, I immediately smiled. Oh how we did our best to keep things as they should be.

Annie Bloom – laughing at the "Duck Hotel". Reconnecting here in Australia in 2016 while you were on tour with Natalie Cole and the WONDERFUL afternoon we spent together. Another instance of the years just melting away.

Karen Krattinger – I always remember your soft southern drawl. Another lovely person I thoroughly enjoyed getting to know.

And then there were...

Morris Day – we were staying at a hotel in Washington DC in order to do a guest appearance at BET. Around 2 in the morning the fire alarm went off. You raced to my door, frantically knocking. I had already learned it was a false alarm but you were taking NO chances. You insisted we take the stairs (elevators not being safe in fires), so down we trudged — 20 floors! We sat in the ice-cold lobby until you were convinced there was no fire. Morning came very early the next day!

Sheila E – the USO tour we did in Turkey and Italy. I have photos of you in the cockpit of the C141 Starlifter as we headed to Turkey's Aviano AFB. Looked like you were all set to navigate!

Jimmy Jam and Terry Lewis – always true gentlemen and graciously invited me to the home of Flyte Tyme Productions for a behind-the-scenes look at their work after The Time.

And "outside" the Paisley family...

Billie Woodruff – I met you when you were just an intern at BET. Without embarrassing you, let's just say you took your love for Prince to heart with your wardrobe. Now you are a highly successful

TV and movie director.

Those are just a few small events that jump to mind. While this may be rather self-indulgent, I felt it important to stress all the good that can come into our lives in the form of the people around us. Perhaps I took for granted that all of these people would be around forever, but of course that's just not how life works.

Remember the moments that matter.

Whenever possible, reach out to those you haven't seen or talked to in a long time. Re-connect!

And, finally...

Acknowledgements can be tricky, not for those you include, but for the ones you inadvertently leave out. With that said, there are just a very few people I need to acknowledge.

PRINCE – what can I say that hasn't been said before? From the incredible music, lyrics, performances and all the things everyone knows about, to what you meant to me and my career.

Paisley Park Wizards – from the people in the offices to the crews, band members, and everyone in between. It was always a joy to work around such professionals who also happened to be pretty terrific people and lifelong friends.

John Staley – for your encouragement and quiet push to get me to put pen to paper.

Celeste Mookherjee – your graphic talents as well as your editing skills made a huge difference in the outcome.

Of course, without the opportunities I was given at Warner Bros. Records, my career would not have been possible.

A Bit About the Author

Marylou Badeaux spent approximately 25 years at Warner Bros. Records in various roles covering marketing and product management in the Black Music Department. She worked with Prince and his organization from the time of his signing in 1978 until 1995 when she moved to the Jazz Department.

In 2001, with the merger of Time-Warner and AOL, she had an opportunity to move to Australia where she has pursued her passions of photography and design.

Marylou is now a recognized book design collaborator for Blurb Publishing. Her specialty is designing photo books of various types, family history books, and other custom designs.

She travels the world for her photography.

http://www.memories4you.com.au

A Bit About the Cover Artist

Mal Bray is an artist, photographer and arts educator living in North Wales, UK.

He has over 40 years of experience of working in commercial art and arts education. Starting as a traditional Illustrator/photographer working in advertising, Mal is now Head of the Art Department at a prestigious Private School in Llandudno, North Wales.

Mal accepts art commissions for a broad range of creative projects and is proficient in traditional illustrative and photographic techniques but also fully embraces contemporary digital approaches.

Mal is happily married to Jane and has two sons – Matthew and Nathan.

https://www.etsy.com/uk/listing/469571189/prince-purple-rain

https://fineartamerica.com/featured/only-want-to-see-you-mal-bray.html

http://malcolm-bray.pixels.com/

CPSIA information can be obtained
at www.ICGtesting.com
Printed in the USA
BVOW05*1945231217

503559BV00017B/331/P

9 780648 189114